Shepherd's Garden Publishing
Felton, California

RECIPES FROM~A KITCHEN GARDEN

VOLUME~TWO

Renee Shepherd and Fran Raboff

Library of Congress Catalog Card Number: 90-92148
ISBN number: 0-9618856-1-0

Published by:
Shepherd's Garden Publishing
7389 West Zayante Road
Felton, CA 95018
(408) 335-5400

Illustrations by Mimi Osborne
Book design by Linda Lane
Typeset in Bembo by Rock & Jones, Oakland, Calif.

First edition

Printed in the United States of America

DEDICATION

To my sister, Susan,
with love and gratitude
for her support in charting
my new life's journey.

ACKNOWLEDGMENTS

Linda Lane's considerable graphic talent has brought grace, sensitivity and solid professional skills to all our joint work. Her artistry has been a major factor in a venture that began as a passion and developed as a life direction.

Mimi Osborne's exceptional talent as an illustrator is obvious to everyone who reads this book. Her extensive horticultural knowledge, attention to detail and meticulous renderings combine with her wit and personal sophistication to make her a marvelous partner.

Dottie Hollinger, my manuscript typist, is actually an equivalent of superwoman, able to accomplish tall stacks of work in a single hour. I am eternally grateful to her for her patience when I leave heaps of handwritten, messy copy on her doorstep late at night and it emerges as perfect-looking, expertly typed copy the very next day, a task I still feel is miraculous even after fifteen years of working with her on projects as diverse as my Ph.D. dissertation and reams of catalog copy, packet backs and this cookbook.

For the past three years, my work has been deeply enhanced by Beth Benjamin, friend, keeper of Alan Chadwick's light, fellow garden lover, flower expert, idea generator, research partner and currently the chief mainstay in keeping the seed catalog on track and enabling me to finish this book!

Many thanks to Al Raboff for his good humor, fine taste buds and endless enthusiasm for testing and tasting sessions while this cookbook was being developed.

Finally, thank you to all the wonderful customers and friends whose visits, letters, comments and enthusiasm underscore the entire process of working on this cookbook.

Contents

Dear Friends

I find that having a kitchen garden provides an ever-expanding palette of colors and tastes to play with, combined with the challenge of finding new ideas for that big rush of ripe zucchini and green beans or the first basket of less familiar new vegetables like radicchio or fennel. Then there is the luxury of fresh herbs at your fingertips, and becoming familiar with all the ways you can use them. These recipes were developed to meet these needs, reflect the natural connection between cooking and gardening, and be an expression of my own personal conviction that growing fresh herbs and vegetables finds a satisfying completion in preparing them well and with pleasure.

Shepherd's Seeds

Our garden seed company offers a wide range of especially fine European, Japanese and domestic vegetable, herb and flower varieties as well as traditional heirlooms. We choose our produce varieties for flavor, tenderness and overall fresh eating qualities and trial them in test gardens in different regions of the country to be sure they'll grow well for everyone. To help our customers enjoy what they grow, we continuously develop recipes so that the pride and satisfaction of offering seeds for the best produce is balanced with lots of ideas on how to really use their harvests on a daily basis. Many of the recipes in this all-new second volume appeared in our most recent catalogs, along with others presented here for the first time.

How Our Garden Grows

I began in my back yard with a series of first sixteen, then twenty-four 3×20-foot boxed raised beds gardened organically in the French Intensive manner. It now also includes a considerable patio garden of pots and containers and another three-year-old quarter-acre garden located next to the horse pasture in our lower field (where we used to play soccer in pre-seed-catalog days). This big lower garden is laid out in a series of long raised beds. Most of the hot-weather and space lovers such as tomatoes, squash, melons, peppers, cucumbers, eggplants and sun-loving flowers have been moved to its sunny location. The original raised-bed backyard garden next to the house still grows all our leafy greens, herbs and brassicas and now includes a permanent herb garden. The herb beds reflect my own initial fascination with different kinds of basils and edible flowers, and the development of my own and our customers' interest in having a continuous supply of many different fresh culinary herbs throughout the gardening seasons. While most of us grew up using dry powdery herbs out of little metal cans or jars, we've seen a real revolution happening as chefs all over the country begin to enhance their cooking with the flavors and scents of fresh herbs. The herb garden also enables us to enjoy the sense of historical continuity provided by centuries-old traditions of herbal lore.

As the seed catalog business has grown and I do more traveling in this country and in Europe to find new seeds and cooking ideas, the head gardening job has inevitably taken on new partners. I now plan and organize the gardens with Wendy Krupnick, a master gardener, who brings with her years of experience with cooking and gardening mentors including chef Jesse Kool and landscape design innovator Rosalind Creasy. Wendy has served as the secretary of the California Certified Organic Growers Organization and her experience and dedication have helped make our gardens' evolution smooth and successful.

The trial gardens continue to expand as I locate new varieties, talk with restaurant folks and visit our home garden customers and gourmet specialty growers. I find that when touring the trials of new cultivars at traditional commercial breeders, I am *still* the only one who evaluates new selections by actually tasting them in addition to evaluating their cultural attributes. (Most commercial seed buyers are interested only in such qualities as uniformity, earliness, etc.) I also actively seek out heirloom vegetables and flowers that may have been preserved in individual gardens or in certain regions of the country for years, but have been being neglected or discontinued by the trade. It is often difficult to find reliable, high-quality seed sources for these treasures, so we've successfully begun to contract for seed production of hard-to-find heirlooms such as Red Russian Kale, Lemon Cucumbers and Opal Basil.

Together Wendy and I carefully lay out our trials of new varieties each fall and spring planting season. We also try to grow many of the current selections we offer in our seed catalog, so visitors can see a "living catalog" of our varieties and we have lots of fine, fresh produce to cook and enjoy. These three functions of trial garden, demonstration garden and working kitchen garden sometimes produce unique dilemmas; for example, we are often faced with needing to harvest all the cinnamon or lemon basil for a recipe-testing session the very same week we have a visiting group coming especially to see the very same herbs in the scented-basil garden area! These challenges keep things interesting all season long.

Cooking Frenzy, Or How We Develop These Recipes

Each spring cooking partner Fran Raboff and I sit down with a list of all the vegetables, herbs and flowers offered in the catalog, a huge pile of customers' and chefs' recipe suggestions, and all the cooking articles and ideas we've saved all year. Twice or three times a week for three or four months we get together for planning, discussion and cooking sessions with the goal of having several finished new recipes for each vegetable and herb each season.

Our cooking sessions begin early in the morning when Fran does the shopping for our ingredient list for that day's seven or eight new dishes and Wendy picks the fresh produce we need from the garden. In the afternoon I arrive (usually late I must admit), feeling much blessed to emerge from our busy office to Fran's large, light and beautifully appointed kitchen. I bring along all the vegetables and herbs Wendy harvested to use from the garden. Fran and I then work our way through the new dishes, changing, testing and inventing as we go. Finally, when all is ready, Fran's husband Al (a truly generous bon vivant and, by the way, a master craftsman of beautiful wooden toys) and invited friends join us for a long and enjoyable testing meal. We have our dinners at her commodious kitchen table overlooking a beautiful view of the grassy and forested hills that surround their mountain retirement home.

As we taste and comment, I keep a stack of the penciled recipes by my side, noting everyone's comments and reactions to each dish. Often Fran or I spring up from the table to see, for example, if the flavor of a salad dressing needs a bit more lemon juice or if a bean dish might be better with a bit more tarragon or a touch more scallion, as everyone gives their suggestions and opinions on how things go together.

Each session produces winners—recipes to retest and probably use in these cookbooks and our catalog—as well as losers (although we always learn something about flavor combinations even on dishes that don't seem special enough to repeat). Then comes the more tedious process of retesting and writing up and checking to make sure everything is just right. Much of the success of this process is due to having Fran's creative skills. She is first and foremost an artist (her acrylic sculptures are magnificent) and having her talents applied to recipe development always expands my cooking horizons.

What We Consider

In creating these recipes, we keep in mind that our readers, like ourselves, are seeking delicious, easy-to-prepare dishes that emphasize fresh ingredients. We try to minimize the use of highly saturated fats and avoid rich sauces while maximizing simplicity of style, wonderful flavors and appetizing presentation. Happily, these goals are easy for fellow home gardeners to achieve; being our own greengrocers we can cook with what is in season at its flavorful best, emphasizing the true honest flavors of tender produce. We also work with our freshly picked herbs to provide subtle flavor accents and succulent fragrance to our dishes. It's especially interesting to do edible flower and herb blossom recipes because although traditions of flower cookery are long and ancient, there is a shortage of modern flower recipes that not only look pretty but taste as good as they look. Fran's expertise with desserts is a real bonus in this area along with her eye for color and fine sense of taste combinations.

Finally

All the recipes in this cookbook have been served with pride and pleasure to my family and friends in many satisfying and memorable meals over the last several seasons. I invite you to enjoy them with us. I want to express my deep appreciation for the many fine recipe ideas shared by our customers. Please continue to send me your feedback and ideas: I look forward to continuing these written conversations, for they are one of the biggest rewards that have grown from my original impulse to share my own enthusiasm and love for the inner and outer joys of cooking from the garden.

VEGETABLES

Fresh vegetables have their very own special allure, and these recipes are first and foremost a celebration of their ingredients. The sweet perfume of a perfectly ripe melon, the silky sheen of deep purple eggplants, the deep rich red of summer tomatoes and the lacy greens and bronzes of lush lettuce rosettes both please the eye and delight the spirit of the gardening cook. Bringing this beautiful abundance into the kitchen presents the delightful challenge of creating dishes to emphasize and enhance the flavors, colors and textures of the harvest. Beauty, freshness and full flavor are our raw materials and these finished dishes are offered in hopes that you will find both satisfaction and joy in their preparation and savor in eating them with your family and friends.

BEANS

CHILLED GREEN BEANS WITH CREAMY HORSERADISH DRESSING

Especially good served as a salad with thick slices of ripe tomatoes.

Cook enough slender green beans to serve 4 to 6 people in salted water until just tender-crisp. Refresh beans with ice water to stop the cooking, drain, pat dry and refrigerate.

Mix together 1 tablespoon horseradish, ½ teaspoon Dijon-style mustard, 2 tablespoons vegetable oil, ⅓ cup sour cream, salt and white pepper to taste. Chill one hour.

Lay the beans on a big serving plate and spoon sauce over them. Serve immediately.

GREEN BEANS IN BASIL-WALNUT VINAIGRETTE

For a lovely presentation, put 1 or 2 radicchio or red cabbage leaves on each salad plate and mound the green beans on top.

1½ pounds young green beans, trimmed
large pan of water

VINAIGRETTE:
1 teaspoon chopped garlic
20 basil leaves
½ teaspoon salt
½ teaspoon freshly ground pepper
2 teaspoons Dijon mustard
4 tablespoons wine vinegar
½ cup oil

GARNISH:
3 scallions thinly sliced
chopped walnuts

Bring water to a rolling boil, add green beans and cook until just tender-crisp. Pour immediately into a colander and pour ice water over them to stop the cooking action. Drain well.

In your blender or food processor put the garlic, basil, salt and ground pepper. Pulse on and off, then add the mustard and vinegar. Pulse until smooth. Add the oil very slowly in a thin stream with the machine running, just until blended.

Place the beans in a serving bowl and pour the vinaigrette over them. Toss to coat thoroughly. Garnish with the scallions and walnuts.

Serves 6 to 8.

GINGERED GREEN BEANS

The piquant flavor of ginger is a natural complement to the taste of fresh beans.

- 1 tablespoon butter (or 1 teaspoon butter and 2 teaspoons oil)
- 1 small onion, very thinly sliced
- 2 teaspoons finely chopped fresh ginger
- ¼ teaspoon crushed fennel seed
- ¼ teaspoon salt
- 1 pound haricots verts or young green beans, tips removed, cut into ½-inch pieces
- ¼ cup chicken broth

Heat butter and oil in a large skillet. Add the onion, ginger, fennel seed and salt. Sauté until onions are glazed and translucent. Add beans and broth. Cover and cook only until beans are tender-crisp.

Serves 4 to 6.

PIA'S ITALIAN COUNTRY BEANS

This dish tastes rich without actually being so.

- 3 tablespoons olive oil
- 2 cloves garlic, finely chopped
- 1 pound green beans, cleaned
- 1 cup beef broth (canned is okay)
- 1 tablespoon fresh parsley, finely chopped
- ¼ cup finely chopped ham or prosciutto

Heat oil and sauté garlic until it becomes fragrant—2 to 3 minutes. Add green beans and sauté 2 to 3 minutes until glossy and well coated. Add broth and cook until beans are just tender-crisp. Sprinkle with chopped parsley and ham and serve.

Serves 4 to 6.

GREEN BEANS WITH TARRAGON

The peppery/anise taste of fresh tarragon pairs beautifully with the vivid flavor of fresh green beans.

- 1 pound green beans, tips removed
- 1 tablespoon olive oil
- 1 tablespoon butter
- 1 small clove garlic, minced
- 3 tablespoons finely chopped scallions
- ⅓ cup thinly sliced celery
- 2 tablespoons finely chopped fresh tarragon or 2 teaspoons dried
- salt and freshly ground pepper

Bring a large pot of salted water to a boil. Put in green beans and cook until just tender-crisp, 3 to 5 minutes. Drain beans in a colander and plunge immediately into ice water to stop the cooking action. Drain on paper towels. Cut beans into 1-inch pieces. Set aside. Heat olive oil and butter in a large skillet. Add garlic, scallions and celery and sauté until softened. Add beans and tarragon; sauté until heated through. Season with salt and fresh pepper to taste.

Serves 4 to 6.

BEETS

LEMON LOVERS' BEETS

The name says it all!

- 1 fresh whole lemon
- 2 tablespoons butter
- 1 tablespoon sugar
- 8 small to medium cooked beets, quartered, or use baby beets
- 1 tablespoon chopped parsley

Grate lemon rind and reserve. Squeeze juice. Melt butter in a saucepan and add the sugar and lemon juice. Cook over moderate heat about 5 minutes or until slightly syrupy. Add the cooked beets and heat through, stirring.

Garnish with the reserved grated lemon rind and chopped parsley and serve.

Serves 2 or 3.

GINGER-ORANGE BEETS

A richly satisfying way to prepare beets that marries several well-matched flavors.

- 6 large beets cooked in their skins until almost tender, cooled
- 1 large orange
- 4 slices bacon cut into ½-inch pieces
- 1 medium onion, diced
- 1 tablespoon grated fresh ginger
- 2 tablespoons light brown sugar
- 2 tablespoons raspberry vinegar
- ½ cup chicken broth or bouillon
- salt and freshly ground pepper
- ½ teaspoon cornstarch dissolved in 1 teaspoon water

Peel and slice beets ¼ to ½ inch thick. Remove the orange zest (thin outer skin only) of the orange. Cut the zest into fine julienne strips. Squeeze the orange—you should have about ½ cup juice. In a deep skillet, cook bacon until golden and almost crisp. Discard most of fat. Add onions and sauté until softened —2 to 3 minutes. Add ginger, brown sugar, orange zest and juice, vinegar and broth and combine. Add beets and cook over low heat for 10 to 15 minutes, stirring frequently. Add salt and pepper to taste. Just before serving, add dissolved cornstarch and water and heat until thickened.

Serves 4.

BROCCOLI

BROCCOLI WITH BUTTERED CRUMBS

These golden crumbs with their hint of pungent rosemary combine perfectly with the robust flavor of fresh broccoli. Another example of simply combining delicious flavors for a fine dish.

- 2 tablespoons butter
- 1 cup fresh bread crumbs
- ¼ cup chopped fresh parsley, packed firmly
- 1 teaspoon minced fresh rosemary or ½ teaspoon dried
- salt and pepper to taste
- 1½ pounds broccoli, cut into florets
- 2 teaspoons melted butter
- 1 tablespoon lemon juice

Melt butter in a heavy skillet over low heat. Add the bread crumbs and cook, stirring constantly, until they are golden-brown. Transfer to a bowl. Blend parsley and rosemary together then combine with the crumbs. Season with salt and pepper. Separately steam the broccoli just until tender-crisp. Remove to a warm serving dish and stir in the melted butter and lemon juice. Salt and pepper to taste. Top with the bread crumb mixture and serve.

Serves 4 to 6.

BRIGHT BROCCOLI SAUTÉ

Eye-catching colors and crisp textures make this a tasty and healthy winner at the table.

- 1 tablespoon olive oil
- 2 large garlic cloves, finely diced
- 1 large onion, halved and very thinly sliced
- 2 red sweet peppers, seeded and cut into thin strips
- 3 cups of broccoli florets cut into bite-size pieces
- 3 tablespoons pine nuts or almonds (toasted lightly if you have time)
- salt and pepper to taste

Heat oil in a large deep skillet. Sauté garlic and onion until soft and translucent. Add peppers and stir-fry for several minutes. Add broccoli and nuts and stir-fry until broccoli is just tender-crisp. Season with salt and pepper to taste and serve right away.

Serves 6.

LEMONY BAKED BROCCOLI

An appetizing and brightly-colored dish that showcases fine fresh broccoli.

> 2 medium heads of broccoli, cut into medium florets with 1-inch stems, about 1¼-1½ pounds total
> 1 teaspoon grated lemon rind
> 2 tablespoons lemon juice
> 2 tablespoons finely chopped fresh parsley
> ¼ cup finely chopped fresh basil
> freshly ground pepper to taste
> ⅓ cup fresh or canned tomato sauce
> 6 thin slices (4 oz.) Mozzarella cheese or one cup grated

Bring a pot of water to a boil and boil or steam the broccoli until it is tender-crisp-done but not over-cooked! Immediately transfer to a bowl of ice water to stop the cooking process and to keep the broccoli bright green. Drain. Put the broccoli into a well-buttered casserole dish and sprinkle with lemon rind, lemon juice, parsley and basil. Add pepper to taste. Spread the tomato sauce over top and cover with the cheese. Bake until hot and bubbly—about 10 minutes at 350°. Serve immediately.

Serves 6.

BROCCOLI WITH PINE NUTS

This recipe shows that less is more—its simplicity yields a delightful dish best made with the freshest broccoli, just harvested from the garden.

> 2 pounds very fresh broccoli
> 1 tablespoon oil
> 2 tablespoons unsalted butter
> 3 tablespoons freshly squeezed lemon juice
> ⅓-½ cup pine nuts, lightly toasted

Divide broccoli into florets about 3 inches long. (Save stems for another dish.) Drop broccoli florets into boiling salted water for a very brief time—no more than 2 minutes, cooking them just until tender-crisp. Drain immediately and put in ice water to stop cooking action. Drain and let dry on a clean kitchen towel or paper toweling.

Heat oil in a skillet, add butter and melt. Whisk in lemon juice. Add the broccoli florets, stir to combine, and sauté for 3 to 5 minutes, turning the broccoli and stirring constantly. Add toasted pine nuts in the last few minutes of cooking and toss with broccoli, combining well to heat the nuts through. Serve immediately.

Serves 4.

Brussels Sprouts

Brussels Sprouts and Corn Crustless Quiche ✓

This recipe brings out the natural sweet nuttiness of both vegetables.

12 brussels sprouts, trimmed and halved
1 tablespoon butter
1½ cups whole milk
2 large eggs
2 tablespoons flour
1 teaspoon salt
1½ teaspoons sugar
½ teaspoon finely chopped fresh oregano, or ¼ teaspoon dried
2 tablespoons finely chopped parsley
¼ teaspoon nutmeg
2 cups cooked, drained corn (frozen corn, thawed okay)
4–5 thinly sliced scallions

Preheat oven to 350°.

Blanch brussels sprouts for one minute in boiling water. Drain and run immediately under cold water to stop cooking. Drain again and place cut-side-down in an 8- or 9-inch casserole dish. Melt the butter in a saucepan, add milk and heat through till warm. In a bowl, beat eggs lightly, then add flour, salt, sugar, herbs and nutmeg. Mix thoroughly, then add corn and scallions. Pour over brussels sprouts. Bake casserole 40–45 minutes and serve hot or at room temperature.

Serves 6.

CABBAGE

BAKED CABBAGE CASSEROLE DINNER ✔

Satisfying and full-flavored but not at all rich.
Makes a whole dinner if combined with crusty bread and a good jug burgundy.

2 tablespoons butter or oil
2 large onions (1 pound) thinly
  sliced
12 ounces mild Italian sausage
3 large tart apples, cored and
  sliced thin
3 tablespoons flour
1 small cabbage, about 1½
  pounds, coarsely shredded
¼ teaspoon salt, divided into
  two portions
freshly ground pepper
¼ teaspoon ground nutmeg,
  divided into two portions
½ cup chicken broth
2 teaspoons lemon juice

TOPPING:
Combine well:
¾ cup bread crumbs
¾ cup coarsely grated sharp
  Cheddar cheese
1 tablespoon minced parsley

Preheat oven to 375°.

Melt butter and sauté onions until softened. Remove from pan and reserve. Remove casing from sausage and sauté until cooked through, breaking up the meat. Drain and reserve. Combine apples with flour. Lightly grease a deep 2½-quart casserole dish. Cover bottom with half of the cabbage, then a layer of half of the apples, half the sausage and half the onions. Sprinkle with half of the salt, pepper to taste, and half of the nutmeg. Repeat with another layer of cabbage, apples, sausage, onions and seasonings. Combine chicken broth and lemon juice and spoon over top. Cover tightly with foil (and casserole lid if available) and bake for 45 to 50 minutes or until tender. Remove foil, sprinkle with crumb topping and bake uncovered for 15 minutes more or until golden and crunchy. Serve hot.

Serves 6.

PICKLED PAK CHOI

A colorful snack—not too tart or too sweet, but crunchy and tasty. Keeps well in the refrigerator for extended enjoyment.

- 2 cups water
- 1 cup red wine vinegar
- ½ cup sugar
- ⅔ cup dry sherry
- 1 teaspoon salt
- 4 large stalks pak choi or 6 to 8 small stalks, cut into ½-inch diagonal slices
- 3 carrots, peeled, and cut into ½-inch diagonal slices
- 3 scallions, cut in 1-inch pieces
- 1 teaspoon mustard seed
- 1 tablespoon finely chopped fresh ginger
- 2 small dried red chile peppers, seeds removed, and coarsely chopped
- optional: 1 clove garlic, halved

In a medium saucepan combine water, vinegar, sugar, sherry and salt. Heat, stirring until sugar is dissolved. Simmer 5 minutes. Remove from heat; cool to room temperature.

Place the prepared vegetables into a 1-quart jar. Stir mustard seed, ginger, red peppers and garlic into cooled vinegar mixture and pour over vegetables. Seal jars with a lid and refrigerate at least 2 days before serving.

Makes 1 quart.

CARROTS

GOLDEN CARROT PIE

The carrots give this delectable pie a beautiful deep persimmon color that makes it even more appetizing.

- 1 unbaked 9-inch pie shell
- 2 pounds carrots thinly sliced (about 7 cups)
- 2 tablespoons butter or margarine
- ⅓ cup brown sugar, firmly packed
- 2 teaspoons grated orange rind
- 1 tablespoon flour
- ½ teaspoon cinnamon
- ½ teaspoon ginger
- ¼ teaspoon nutmeg
- pinch of salt
- 2 eggs
- 1 cup evaporated milk
- 1 teaspoon vanilla

Preheat oven to 425°.

Steam carrots until very tender. Purée in a food processor or blender. Then add butter, brown sugar and orange rind. Add to this mixture the flour, cinnamon, ginger, nutmeg and salt. Blend well. When mixture has cooled, beat in eggs, evaporated milk and vanilla, mixing just until combined. Pour into pie shell. Bake in the lower third of the oven 20 minutes, then reduce heat to 350° and bake 45 minutes longer or until a knife inserted near the edge comes out clean. Cool on rack.

Serves 6 to 8.

CARROT BRAN MUFFINS ✓

Fine and rich tasting with the extra nutrition and goodness of sweet carrots.

- 1½ cups flour
- 1½ teaspoons baking powder
- ½ teaspoon baking soda
- 1 teaspoon cinnamon
- ¼ teaspoon nutmeg
- ¼ teaspoon salt
- 1¼ cups bran
- ½ cup currants
- 2 eggs
- ⅔ cup firmly packed dark brown sugar
- ½ cup vegetable oil
- 1½ cups finely grated carrots
- 1 cup buttermilk
- 1 teaspoon vanilla
- 6 dates cut in half to make 12 halves

Preheat oven to 350°.

Sift together the flour, baking powder, baking soda, cinnamon, nutmeg, and salt. Stir in bran and currants. Set aside. In a large bowl beat eggs lightly; add brown sugar, vegetable oil, carrots, buttermilk and vanilla, mixing until well blended. Add the dry ingredients into the egg mixture, mixing just until combined. Do not over-mix. Spoon into greased muffin tins, filling them two-thirds full; top each with a date half. Bake 25–30 minutes until muffins pull away from sides of the pan.

Makes 12–14 muffins.

PICKLED BABY CARROTS

Especially nice made with our round baby carrots.

- 1 pound freshly picked baby carrots
- 2 cups water
- ½ cup wine vinegar
- 1 teaspoon each: salt, mustard seed, and peppercorns
- 1 bay leaf
- 1 tablespoon sugar

Trim carrots at both ends and scrub well. Combine carrots with remaining ingredients and cook 6 to 8 minutes until tender but still crisp. (Cooking time will depend on the size of carrots.) Cool the carrots in the liquid, then drain and chill in glass jar(s) in the refrigerator. They will keep nicely for a week to ten days in the refrigerator (if you don't eat them all first).

Makes approximately one pint.

Carrots with Lemon and Dill

Dill and carrots not only look well together but taste terrific when paired up.

> 1 pound carrots cut into ½-inch slices
> 2 tablespoons butter
> ½ cup minced onion (1 small)
> ¼ cup dry white wine
> ½ teaspoon grated lemon rind
> 1 to 2 tablespoons lemon juice
> 2 tablespoons minced fresh dill weed
> salt and white pepper

Steam carrots for about seven minutes until tender crisp. In a skillet, heat butter until foamy; add onion and sauté until softened. Add carrots, wine, lemon rind and one tablespoon of the lemon juice, and cook stirring until most of the liquid is reduced, about 2 minutes. Add the dill, salt and white pepper and additional lemon juice to taste. Serve hot.

Serves 4.

Carrots with Lime Butter Sauce

A tropical touch of lime enhances tender-crisp carrots.

> 2 tablespoons butter
> 2 scallions, chopped
> 1 pound carrots, cut in ½-inch chunks
> grated green rind (zest) of one lime
> juice of one lime to equal 1 tablespoon
> salt and papper to taste
> 2 tablespoons chopped parsley
> optional garnish: 2 tablespoons very finely chopped nuts

Melt butter in a large skillet. Add scallions and carrots and sauté together two to three minutes. Add lime rind and juice, cover and cook over low heat until carrots are just tender-crisp. Add salt and pepper to taste. Garnish with chopped parsley, adding nuts if desired.

Serves 4 to 6.

CAULIFLOWER

CRUMBLE-TOPPED CAULIFLOWER

The smoothness of the cauliflower matches up well with this tasty crumble topping.

1 head cauliflower, broken into
  florets
2 tablespoons olive oil
2 tablespoons butter
2 hard-boiled eggs, finely
  chopped
¾ teaspoon ground cumin
⅓ cup bread crumbs
¼ cup Parmesan cheese
salt and pepper to taste
3 tablespoons finely chopped
  parsley

Drop cauliflower florets into a saucepan of boiling water and cook just until tender—3 to 5 minutes. Drain. Melt the oil and butter in a skillet, add cauliflower and stir briefly, just until pieces begin to color. Mix together all other ingredients and spread over top of cauliflower. Heat through so cheese melts, then serve right away.

Serves 4.

YOGURT CURRIED CAULIFLOWER

The creamy cauliflower combines perfectly with the smooth yogurt and curry sauce.

1 large head cauliflower, washed
1 tablespoon butter
1 cup *fresh* plain yogurt
½ teaspoon good curry powder
2 teaspoons seasoned bread
  crumbs

Steam the cauliflower whole just until tender. Do not overcook! Remove the cauliflower carefully to serving plate and dot with butter. Combine the yogurt and curry powder and spread over the cauliflower. Sprinkle with bread crumbs and serve promptly.

Serves 4 to 6.

CHARD

MILANESE STYLE CHARD √

A fine northern Italian dish that marries chard's full flavor with a delicious herb-based sauce.

1 bunch (1 pound) swiss chard, trimmed of coarse stems and coarsely chopped
2 tablespoons olive oil
1 clove garlic, minced
6 scallions including green tops, thinly sliced
2 tablespoons chopped fresh parsley
¼ cup chopped fresh basil
pinch nutmeg
¼ cup chopped prosciutto or ham
2 tablespoons freshly grated Parmesan cheese
salt and freshly ground pepper

GARNISH:
2 tablespoons toasted pine nuts or chopped walnuts

In a large deep skillet heat olive oil, add garlic and scallions and sauté until softened and fragrant, 2 to 3 minutes. Add chard, parsley, basil, nutmeg, prosciutto or ham and mix together well. Cover the skillet and cook over medium heat until tender and wilted, 3 to 5 minutes. Mix in Parmesan cheese and then add salt and pepper to taste. Serve garnished with the pine nuts or walnuts.

Serves 4 to 6.

JUICY SAUTÉED SWISS CHARD

A wonderfully easy way to make chard into one of your family's most favored vegetables.

1 bunch (1 pound) swiss chard, trimmed of tough stems and chopped coarsely
2 tablespoons olive oil
1 clove garlic, minced
6 scallions including green tops, thinly sliced
2 medium tomatoes, peeled, diced and drained
2 tablespoons red wine vinegar
2 teaspoons sugar
⅛ teaspoon Tabasco sauce
¼ cup chopped fresh basil
¼ cup sour cream ("low fat" okay)
salt and freshly ground pepper

Trim chard, discarding tough or woody stems. In a large skillet, heat olive oil, add garlic and scallions and sauté until softened, 2 to 3 minutes. Add chard, tossing to coat leaves. Cover pan with a lid and heat for 3 to 5 minutes until chard is wilted and tender. Add tomatoes, vinegar, sugar, Tabasco sauce and basil. Heat through for 2 to 3 minutes. Remove from stove and mix in sour cream. Add salt and pepper to taste and serve.

Serves 4 to 6.

CHARD WITH BEET VINEGAR

The colorful, vibrant sweet-and-sour sauce combines with the smooth finish of sour cream to really set off the flavor of the chard.

2 large cooked beets, peeled
1 cup rice vinegar
3 tablespoons sugar
½ teaspoon lemon juice
dash white pepper
1 large bunch fresh chard or beet greens, washed and chopped
butter

GARNISH:
sour cream or fresh plain yogurt

In a blender, purée the beets together with the rice vinegar, sugar, lemon juice and white pepper. Pour into a non-aluminum saucepan and bring to a boil. Reduce heat and simmer covered five minutes. Cool. Steam the chard until tender, drain. Toss chard with butter and pepper to taste. Arrange the cooked chard on a serving platter. Spoon over some of the beet vinegar (to taste) and garnish with a very generous dollop of sour cream or yogurt.

Serves 4.

CORN

FRESH CORN MUFFINS

Especially good served hot with honey.

- 1⅓ cups unbleached all-purpose flour
- 2½ teaspoons baking powder
- ½ teaspoon baking soda
- ½ teaspoon salt
- 3 tablespoons sugar
- ⅔ cup corn meal
- 2 eggs lightly beaten
- 1 cup buttermilk or fresh plain yogurt
- 2 tablespoons melted butter
- 1 cup cooked corn kernels—about 1 large ear

Preheat oven to 375° and lightly grease 12 muffin cups. Sift together the flour, baking powder, baking soda, salt and sugar. Mix in cornmeal. In a separate bowl, combine beaten eggs with the buttermilk (or yogurt), melted butter and corn. Combine these wet ingredients with the dry ingredients, mixing just until blended; don't overmix. Spoon into muffin tins. Bake 20–25 minutes, until a cake tester inserted in center comes out clean.

Makes 12 muffins.

DRIED CORN SNACK

For the corn-rich cook, this chewy and nutty-sweet natural snack is perfect for munching while watching fall games.

- 8 large ears of fresh corn cut from the cob, about 7–8 cups
- 3 tablespoons sugar
- 2 teaspoons salt
- ¼ cup milk

Combine corn, sugar, salt and milk in a heavy-bottomed saucepan. Bring to a boil, then lower to simmer and cook for 15 minutes, stirring frequently. Pour into a shallow greased baking pan and dry in a low, 250° oven for about 1½ hours, stirring occasionally. Corn should be light golden brown when done. Store in covered container for snacking.

FRESH TOMATO CORN SOUP

The combined flavors of fresh sweet corn, tomatoes and herbs is unbeatable in this simple light soup.

1 tablespoon butter
1 tablespoon olive oil
1½ cups chopped onions (about 2 medium)
2 pounds fresh tomatoes, peeled and coarsely chopped
1½ tablespoons tomato paste
4 cups chicken broth
1 teaspoon chopped fresh thyme or ½ teaspoon dried
1 teaspoon chopped fresh dill or ½ teaspoon dried
¼ cup packed fresh basil, chopped
2 cups fresh corn kernels
salt and white pepper to taste

In large saucepan heat butter and olive oil, add onion and sauté until softened. Add tomatoes, tomato paste and chicken broth. Bring to a boil, reduce heat and simmer the mixture for 30–40 minutes until vegetables are tender. In a blender purée mixture in batches. Return to saucepan, add herbs and corn and cook 5 minutes longer. Add salt and pepper to taste.

Serves 6 to 8.

BLACK BEAN AND FRESH CORN SALAD

Fine-tasting and colorful, the textures and flavors of this inviting salad are splendid together.

2 cups cooked or canned black beans, drained
2 cups briefly cooked corn kernels, drained
2 tomatoes, peeled, seeded, diced
½ red bell pepper, diced
½ green bell pepper, diced
4 scallions, sliced
3 tablespoons minced cilantro
2 tablespoons red wine vinegar
½ teaspoon ground cumin
⅛ teaspoon red pepper flakes
3 tablespoons olive oil
salt and freshly ground pepper to taste

GARNISH:
parsley or cilantro

Mix all the ingredients together about an hour before serving to blend flavors. Add salt and pepper to taste. Garnish and serve on lettuce as individual salads or as a colorful relish/salad with buffet dinners.

Makes 5 to 6 cups.

CUCUMBERS

ISRAELI CUCUMBER SALAD ✓

A creamy, crunchy and aromatic summer salad we think you'll make often. Great for Saturday supper after a full day.

4 scallions, cut into 1-inch lengths
¼ teaspoon salt
juice of one lemon, freshly squeezed
1 large cucumber, peeled and thinly sliced
1 bunch red radishes (8 to 10), thinly sliced
½ cup sour cream (don't substitute)
1 tablespoon chopped chives

Put the scallions and salt in a glass or wooden bowl, then use the edge and bottom of a heavy drinking glass to smash the scallion and salt thoroughly. Add the lemon juice and mix thoroughly. Add the cucumber and radishes; mix well. Add sour cream and mix well. Garnish with chopped chives and serve.

Serves 4.

CHILLED CUCUMBER BORSHT

Jewel-like colors and fresh full flavor give real meaning to the term "appetizer."

8 small peeled beets, cooked in water to cover until tender; reserve cooking water
1 scallion, chopped
1½ cups seeded, peeled cucumber, chopped
1 cup buttermilk
1 tablespoon wine vinegar
⅛ teaspoon sugar
1½ teaspoons fresh lemon juice
salt and pepper to taste
3 tablespoons fresh dill, finely chopped
2 tablespoons fresh chives, finely chopped

In a blender, purée the beets and water they were cooked in, scallion, half the cucumbers, and the buttermilk, vinegar, sugar, and lemon juice. Add salt and pepper to taste. Transfer to a serving bowl. Add remaining cucumber and sprinkle with dill and chives. Serve chilled.

Serves 4.

DANISH CUCUMBER SALAD ✓

Made with fresh dill and sweet, crunchy cucumbers, this light salad is really addicting; it goes well with both light suppers and big buffet dinners in hot summer weather.

> 3 large cucumbers, peeled
> salt
> ⅔ cup white vinegar
> ½ cup water
> ½ cup sugar
> ½ teaspoon salt
> ¼ teaspoon white pepper
> 2 tablespoons chopped fresh dill
>   leaf or 1 tablespoon dried
>
> GARNISH:
> red or yellow cherry tomatoes

Slice cucumbers very thin. Arrange them in layers in a non-aluminum bowl, sprinkling each layer with salt. Put a plate on top of the cucumbers and a heavy weight over the dish. Let them remain at room temperature for several hours or overnight in the refrigerator.

Drain cucumbers thoroughly. Pat dry on paper towels. Return to a bowl. In a small skillet heat to a boil the vinegar, water, sugar, salt and pepper. Reduce the heat and simmer 3 minutes, stirring until the sugar is dissolved. Pour the hot mixture over the cucumbers. Sprinkle with the chopped dill. Chill for 3 to 4 hours. Drain cucumbers and serve in a pretty glass bowl surrounded by the cherry tomatoes.

Serves 6 to 8.

CHINESE CUCUMBER SALAD ✓

This delicate, well-balanced marinade shows off fresh cucumbers at their best.

> 3 cups cucumbers, rinds scored
>   or peeled, sliced very thin
> ½ teaspoon salt
> ¼ teaspoon sugar
> 2 teaspoons white wine vinegar
>
> DRESSING:
> ½ teaspoon grated fresh ginger
> 1 teaspoon soy sauce
> ¼ teaspoon sugar
> 1 tablespoon white wine vinegar
> 2 tablespoons vegetable oil
> 1 tablespoon chopped chives
> 1 tablespoon chopped red bell
>   pepper
> ⅛ teaspoon red chili pepper
>   flakes
> salt and pepper to taste

Put cucumber in a bowl with salt, sugar and vinegar. Toss and let stand 30 minutes. Drain, chill 30 minutes, and drain again. Combine dressing ingredients. Toss with drained cucumbers. Season with salt and pepper to taste.

Serves 4.

Eggplant

Baked Eggplant with Feta Cheese

An easy appetizer or whole meal for eggplant lovers.

> **1 large or 2 medium eggplants**
> **olive oil**
> **⅓ cup feta cheese (Gorgonzola is another alternative, if you love it)**
> **¼ cup finely chopped fresh basil, packed in cup to measure**

Preheat oven to 350°.

Slice eggplant into ½-inch slices. Brush slices with olive oil and grill or broil until lightly browned on one side. Turn slices over and brush other side with oil. Arrange slices on an oiled baking sheet. Sprinkle the cheese over the slices. Bake 10 minutes or until cheese is bubbly and eggplant slices are soft. Sprinkle fresh chopped basil over the top of the eggplant slices and serve hot.

Serves 4 to 6.

Sweet and Sour Eggplant

Quick and tasty, without using too much oil.

Use 2 medium eggplants. Cut into ½-inch slices. Then quarter the slices. Salt and let drain for 30 minutes. Then rinse off and pat dry. Put 2 tablespoons of olive oil in a heavy skillet and add eggplant. Sauté until tender (8–10 minutes). Sprinkle with 2 tablespoons sugar, turn over the slices and cook briefly until they begin to caramelize. Add 2 tablespoons red wine vinegar. Stir to blend. Serve immediately. *Optional:* Add 1 small finely minced clove garlic when sautéing eggplant.

Serves 4.

Caponata
(Cold Eggplant Appetizer)

A wonderful, rich-tasting appetizer, long part of traditional Italian cuisine and well worth making. Here is our version.

1 large or 2 smaller eggplants (about 2 pounds total) cut into 1-inch cubes
½ cup olive oil
2 cloves garlic, finely chopped
2 large onions, finely chopped
1 green or red sweet pepper, seeded and chopped
enough fresh ripe tomatoes, peeled and chunked, to make 3 cups
⅓ cup red wine vinegar
2 tablespoons sugar
2 tablespoons tomato sauce
½ cup green or black olives, cut in halves
3 tablespoons drained capers
⅓ cup fresh basil finely chopped or 2 tablespoons dried
2 tablespoons chopped parsley
salt and pepper to taste
optional: 2 tablespoons slivered almonds or whole pine nuts

In a large heavy skillet, heat ¼ cup of the olive oil. Add eggplant cubes and sauté over medium high heat, stirring and turning constantly for about 8 minutes, or until they are lightly browned. Remove to a bowl.

Pour the remaining ¼ cup of olive oil into the skillet, heat oil, add garlic, onion, and green peppers and sauté another 3 to 4 minutes or until softened. Add tomatoes and simmer 10 minutes over low heat, stirring frequently.

In a small saucepan heat vinegar and sugar together over a high heat until part of vinegar evaporates slightly, 2 to 3 minutes. Add to large skillet with onion mixture. Return eggplant to skillet along with tomato sauce mixture, olives, and capers and simmer uncovered, stirring frequently, for about 15 minutes. Stir in basil, parsley, salt and pepper to taste. Add a little extra vinegar if necessary. Stir in nuts if used and heat through for 5 minutes longer. Transfer to a serving dish. Stores very well in refrigerator.

Serve hot or cold with crackers.

Serves 12 to 14 as an appetizer.

BROILED TURKISH EGGPLANT

A striking dish that makes a show-off appetizer, first course or luncheon dish.

2 medium-sized eggplants, unpeeled
olive or salad oil
1 tablespoon butter
1 large clove garlic, minced
2 tablespoons chopped fresh basil
3 or 4 ripe tomatoes, chopped
½ teaspoon sugar
salt to taste
1 cup fresh plain yogurt or sour cream

GARNISH:
chopped chives or scallions

Slice the eggplant into ½-inch slices. Brush both sides of each slice with oil and broil them on both sides until soft and slightly browned. (Watch closely as slices cook quickly!)

Prepare a simple tomato sauce: In a heavy saucepan melt butter and add the minced garlic. Cook for one minute and add the basil and the tomatoes. Stir and cook down until they reach a fairly thick sauce consistency. Add the sugar, stir and remove from heat; let cool slightly. Salt to taste.

On each serving plate, lay a slice of eggplant. Top with the tomato sauce but leave the outer edges of each slice showing—don't cover the slice completely. Finish by adding a generous tablespoon of fresh yogurt or sour cream in the center of the slice. Sprinkle with chopped chives or scallions.

Serves 8.

FENNEL

FENNEL BRAISED IN VERMOUTH

The aromatic braising liquid deepens fennel's delicate flavor.

2 tablespoons olive oil
1 small onion, finely chopped
½ clove garlic
2 large bulbs fennel, sliced into ½-inch slices
2 tablespoons finely chopped leafy fennel tops
¾ cup dry vermouth
⅓ cup half-and-half or cream
salt and pepper to taste
½ cup freshly grated Parmesan or Asiago cheese

Heat oil in large deep skillet and sauté onion and garlic until softened, about 3 minutes. Add sliced fennel and toss until glazed, 2 to 3 minutes. Add vermouth and braise the fennel until tender-crisp—about 8 minutes. Add the minced fennel tops, the half-and-half, salt and pepper and cook another 4 to 5 minutes to reduce and slightly thicken the sauce. Sprinkle with grated cheese; serve immediately.

Serves 4.

KALE

HEARTY PORTUGUESE KALE SOUP

On a cold and wet fall night, serve this soup with warm crusty bread and beer or red wine for a complete and satisfying hot meal.

1 tablespoon olive oil
½ pound of your favorite smoked sausage, sliced about ½ inch thick
4 cups chicken broth
1 medium onion, thinly sliced
3 medium potatoes, thinly sliced
1 large bunch or about 1 pound kale, shredded or sliced up very thin
optional: salt and pepper

Heat the oil in a skillet and sauté the sausage just until the fat is rendered —3 to 5 minutes. Drain on paper towels and reserve. Bring the broth to a boil with the onion and the potatoes and simmer 10 to 15 minutes until the potatoes are very tender. Mash the onions and potatoes in the broth with a potato masher or slotted spoon. Add the drained sausage slices and the kale. Bring back to a boil and then simmer 4 to 6 minutes until the kale is tender. Taste for seasoning—depending on how spicy your sausage is, add salt and pepper to taste.

Serves 4 to 6.

AUSTRIAN KALE

A traditional and delicious side dish for roast pork, beef, or chicken.

2 bunches washed kale
1 clove garlic
½ medium onion, coarsely chopped
1 tablespoon oil
1½ cups chicken stock or bouillon
4 medium-sized potatoes, quartered
1 stalk chopped celery

GARNISH:
sour cream

Cut the kale leaves into ½-inch-wide strips. Blanch them in lightly salted boiling water for one minute. Set aside. Sauté the garlic and onion in the oil until lightly browned. Add the chicken stock, potatoes, celery, and blanched kale. Simmer together until potatoes fall apart and lose their shape. Stir; season with salt and pepper and serve.

Serves 4 to 6.

LEEKS

LEMONY LEEK SOUP ✓

The subtle flavors of the lemon, herbs and leeks combine perfectly in this silky smooth soup. Makes a memorable first course or a complete lunch.

1 tablespoon butter or margarine
2 tablespoons vegetable oil
6 cups (about 6 to 8) thinly sliced
   leeks
1 carrot, thinly sliced
1 stalk celery, thinly sliced
6 cups chicken broth
1 tablespoon grated lemon rind
2 tablespoons lemon juice
2 teaspoons fresh marjoram or
   1 teaspoon dried
1 tablespoon chopped parsley
¼ cup rice
½ cup milk
salt and white pepper to taste

GARNISH:
sour cream or yogurt
3 tablespoons minced chives

In a 4- to 5-quart saucepan, heat butter and oil, add leeks, carrot and celery, and sauté until softened. Add chicken broth, lemon rind, lemon juice, marjoram, parsley and rice and simmer covered for about 40 minutes until vegetables are very tender. Purée in batches in a blender or food processor. Pour mixture back into saucepan; add milk, salt and pepper to taste. If soup is too thick add extra milk or broth. Heat soup through, but do not boil. Serve hot or cold, sprinkled with chives and a dollop of sour cream or yogurt. Makes about 7½ cups.

Serves 6 to 8.

BRAISED AND GLAZED LEEKS ✓

The succulent leeks braise slowly to perfection in this dish.

6 to 8 medium to large leeks
2 tablespoons olive oil
2 cloves garlic, minced
1 tablespoon water
1 teaspoon sugar
3 tablespoons wine vinegar
salt and freshly ground pepper
2 tablespoons parsley, finely
   chopped

Trim tops off leeks, leaving 1 inch of the green tops. Cut larger leeks into 1-inch slices, the smaller ones into 1½-inch pieces. In a large skillet heat oil. Add garlic and sauté until softened. Add the leeks and toss to coat them with oil. Arrange the leeks in a single layer in a skillet. Add 1 tablespoon water. Cover pan and cook at *very* low heat for 20–25 minutes, shaking pan occasionally to keep them from sticking. When leeks are tender, turn up heat and sprinkle with sugar and vinegar. Stir gently until the leeks are glazed with the syrupy mixture. Season with salt and pepper; add parsley and serve.

Serves 4 to 6.

LEEKS VICTOR ✔

A new adaptation of a classic recipe for celery that works beautifully for leeks, enhancing their sweet and mild onion flavor.

DRESSING:
3 tablespoons fresh lemon juice
1 teaspoon Dijon mustard
⅛ teaspoon sugar
2 tablespoons chopped fresh
  parsley
2 tablespoons sweet pickle relish
¼ cup light olive oil
salt and pepper to taste

LEEKS:
4 to 6 leeks, ½ to ⅓ inches in
  diameter
2 to 3 cups rich chicken or beef
  broth
1 hard–boiled egg, finely chopped

**optional but traditional: 1 two–
  ounce can of anchovy filets,
  drained and rinsed**

Combine and blend all dressing ingredients. Set aside. Trim the leeks, leaving 2 inches of green leaves. Discard outer layer of leeks and cut off the root ends. Split each leek in half lengthwise; wash well. Place leeks in a deep skillet or sauce-pan large enough to hold them in one layer and cover with chicken broth. Bring to a boil, then reduce heat and slowly simmer for about 15 minutes or until tender. With a slotted spoon, transfer leeks to a dish, again in a single layer. (Save the savory broth for another use.) Stir then pour the dressing over the hot leeks; salt and pepper to taste. Allow the dish to cool and flavors to blend for at least several hours, basting occasionally. Top with chopped eggs and/or anchovy filets, and serve as a side dish or on lettuce leaves as a salad.

Serves 4 to 6.

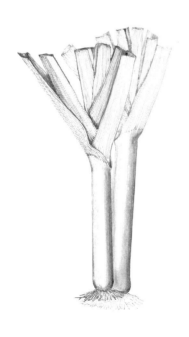

37

MELONS

MAMA SIMON'S PICKLED WATERMELON RIND

Our family recipe for this old-fashioned sweet pickle. Made from scratch,
it bears little resemblance to store-bought versions! Especially good to take on picnics.
Use like sweet pickles or chutney. Stores well in refrigerator.

7 pounds of watermelon rind,
leaving on a bit of pink flesh
(about ¼ inch)
1 tablespoon salt
6 lemons, washed
4 oranges, washed
3 cups white sugar
3 cups brown sugar
3 cinnamon sticks
6 whole peppercorns
4 teaspoons whole cloves
1 quart cider or other mild
vinegar
1 cup water
½ pound candied ginger, chopped
fresh washed and dried whole
grape leaves (this is the natural
way to keep pickles crispy)

Peel green outer layer from melon
rind. Cut rind into 1- to 2-inch
cubes. Put in a large saucepan, cover
with cold water, add salt and bring
to a boil, then turn down to a simmer
and cook until the rind is tender but
still crispy. Drain the rind and stop
the cooking by dropping it into ice-
water. Drain and pat dry.

Squeeze the juice from the lemons
and oranges and reserve. Cut their
rinds into strips and remove pith.

Put rind strips in a pan. Cover with
cold water, bring to a boil, then
pour out the water. Repeat, boiling
up the rind for a total of 3 times.
(Start with cold water each time.)

In a large saucepan mix the sugars;
add cinnamon, peppercorns, cloves,
vinegar, water, ginger, and lemon
and orange juice. Heat, stirring,
until sugar is dissolved. Cook about
30 minutes at medium heat or until
reduced and slightly syrupy. Add
reserved watermelon rind and lemon
and orange rinds. Simmer gently for
about 30 minutes or until the watermelon rind appears translucent.

Remove fruit with slotted spoon.
Put a grape leaf in bottom of each jar
and fill with rind, leaving one inch
headroom. Cook remaining syrup
down until slightly thickened, then
pour over the rinds in the jars. Complete the seals if desired and process
jars in hot-water bath for 20 minutes.
Or store jars in refrigerator.

Makes 8 pints.

MELON AND STRAWBERRIES WITH CRUNCHY STREUSEL TOPPING

A light, really scrumptious dessert. The fast run under the broiler seems to enhance the fresh fruits' flavor.

    5 cups cubed melon combined with 2 cups halved ripe strawberries, both at room temperature
    4 teaspoons orange juice
    1 eight-ounce carton of very fresh plain yogurt, drained

    STREUSEL TOPPING:
    ½ cup cookie or graham cracker crumbs
    ½ cup dark brown sugar, packed
    ¼ cup flour
    2 pinches of ground nutmeg
    ½ cup chopped nuts
    ¼ cup butter

Preheat broiler, spread the fruits in the bottom of a baking pan and sprinkle the orange juice evenly over them. Spread the yogurt evenly over the fruit in a thin layer. Combine Streusel Topping ingredients, adding butter last, and blend just until crumbly, but do not overmix. Sprinkle topping mixture over yogurt.

Run the pan under a preheated broiler for about two minutes, watching closely. Serve warm. Don't expect leftovers!

Serves 6.

MELON MERINGUE

Light, elegant to serve, and fun to make for a not-too-rich grand finale.

    2 cantaloupes or Charentais melons, flesh cut into 1-inch cubes (or use a melon ball cutter)
    ⅓ cup melon or citrus flavored liqueur
    2 teaspoons grated orange rind
    ⅓ cup plus 1 tablespoon sugar
    3 large egg whites at room temperature
    ¼ teaspoon cream of tartar
    3 tablespoons sliced toasted almonds
    2 tablespoons powdered sugar

Preheat oven to 500°.

In a large baking dish or pretty ovenproof casserole, combine the melon with the liqueur, orange rind and 1 tablespoon of the sugar and mix together gently but thoroughly. Let marinate for 15 to 30 minutes.

In a large bowl, beat the egg whites with an electric mixer on high speed. When they are foamy, add the cream of tartar and beat until soft peaks form. Gradually add the ⅓ cup of remaining granulated sugar and continue beating just until the whites hold stiff moist peaks. Spoon the beaten egg-white mixture over the center of the melon pieces. Sprinkle evenly with nuts and powdered sugar. Bake only until the top is a light golden brown; about 4 or 5 minutes. Serve right away as a splendid dessert.

Serves 6.

ONIONS

BREAD AND BUTTER PICKLED ONIONS

Mild, crunchy and especially good with cold cuts, cold chicken or tuna. Stores well in the refrigerator, too.

**Approximately 3 pounds or 6
   medium onions**

BRINE MIXTURE:
1 cup white vinegar
2 quarts water
1 tablespoon salt

PICKLING MIXTURE:
2 cups white vinegar
2 cups sugar
1 tablespoon salt
3 tablespoons mustard seed
1 tablespoon celery seed
¼ teaspoon curry powder

8 eight-ounce or 4 pint glass jars

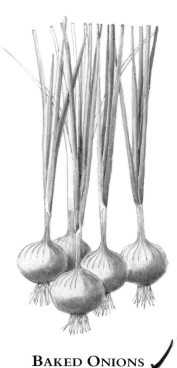

Peel onions, cut in half crosswise, then into ¼-inch strips. Separate onions into strips and place in a bowl, covering with brine mixture. Let stand several hours or overnight.
   In a 4- or 5-quart saucepan, combine pickling ingredients and bring to a boil over medium heat, stirring until sugar is dissolved. Boil 2 minutes. Remove the onion strips from the brine, draining well. Add them to the hot pickling mixture and boil for one minute. Pack the onions in clean glass jars and cover them with the hot pickling mix, leaving ½-inch head space before sealing with two-piece lids. Store in refrigerator for a week, allowing flavors to blend.

**Makes about 8 eight-ounce jars or 4
pints. Stores well in refrigerator.**

BAKED ONIONS

As good as baked potatoes and just as easy.

4 large whole onions, peeled
2 tablespoons softened butter
**1 tablespoon fresh thyme (or
   1 teaspoon dried)**
salt and pepper
foil

Preheat oven to 375°.
   Slice off and discard the top ½-inch of the stem end of each onion. Spread the cut surfaces with butter and sprinkle with thyme, salt and pepper. Place each onion on a square of foil, large enough to completely enclose it. Wrap each onion up tightly and put in preheated oven. Bake about 1 hour. Let each diner unwrap his or her own baked onion.

Serves 4.

PARSLEY

PARSLEY ANTIPASTO SALAD

A mouthwatering and sprightly first-course salad, bright with color and flavor.

> 1 clove garlic, minced and
>   mashed to a paste
> 3 tablespoons fresh lemon juice
> ¼ cup olive oil
> salt and pepper
> ¼ cup Swiss cheese, cut into
>   very small cubes
> ½ cup pecan pieces, chopped
> ½ cup flat-leaved parsley, finely
>   chopped
> ¼ cup quartered olives
> ¼ cup chopped sweet red or
>   yellow pepper
> 1 scallion, finely chopped
> optional: ¼ cup finely chopped
>   sun-dried tomatoes
> large lettuce leaves for 4 salad
>   plates

> **GARNISH:**
> **parsley sprigs and lemon slices**

Combine the garlic and lemon juice and add the oil in a stream, whisking the dressing until it is blended. Add salt and pepper to taste. Stir in the cheese, nuts, parsley, olives, chopped pepper, scallion and dried tomatoes if used. Garnish and serve on lettuce-lined plates.

Serves 4.

GREMOLATA

A traditional Italian condiment, we love it as a quick and healthy topping for lightly buttered baked potatoes, plain broiled chicken, or any mild-flavored baked fish or veal dish.

> ⅔ cup finely chopped fresh
>   parsley
> 2 cloves garlic, finely chopped
> 1½ tablespoons grated lemon
>   rind

Combine and mix all ingredients together thoroughly. Best if made at least 30 minutes in advance to allow flavors to blend.

Makes ⅔ cup.

Linguini with Fresh Parsley Clam Sauce

A smooth, creamy and delicious quick sauce; parsley and clams just seem to go together.

2 small cloves of garlic, minced
2 or 3 scallions, finely chopped
1 to 2 tablespoons olive oil
2 six-ounce cans chopped clams
1 cup half-and-half (or use whole milk)
1 cup fresh parsley, finely chopped
1 cup fresh grated Parmesan or Asiago cheese
salt and pepper to taste
8 ounces linguini noodles

GARNISH:
1 large tomato, seeded, drained and coarsely chopped
juice of ½ lemon

Sauté garlic and scallions in olive oil until soft. Add clam juice from canned clams and the half-and-half and simmer until reduced and thickened, 8 to 10 minutes. Stir in clams and parsley and simmer another 5 minutes. Add cheese, stir, and add salt and pepper to taste. Cook the linguini in boiling, salted water and drain. Heat sauce through and mix with hot linguini. Garnish with chopped tomato and sprinkle lemon juice over the top. Serve immediately, piping hot.

Serves 4 to 6.

Garbanzo Bean and Parsley Dip

The addition of fresh parsley freshens and finishes the nutty, mild beans in this version of a '60s standard we all enjoy often.

15½ ounce can garbanzo beans (drained, reserving liquid) or 1¾ cups cooked beans
1 clove garlic, minced
3 tablespoons lemon juice
⅓ cup tahini (sesame seed paste)
2 scallions, chopped
½ teaspoon ground cumin
¼ teaspoon soy sauce
½ cup chopped parsley
salt, pepper and a pinch of cayenne

GARNISH:
Chopped fresh mint and/or parsley leaves

In a food processor or blender combine beans, ¼ cup of the bean liquid, garlic, lemon juice, tahini, scallions, cumin, soy sauce and parsley. Process until mixture is smooth. (If mixture seems too thick, add a little extra garbanzo bean liquid.) Taste for seasoning, adding salt, pepper and cayenne.

Serve with pita bread triangles or crispy crackers.

Serves 6 to 8.

Peas

Gingered Peas and Yellow Squash

Perfumed and colorful, this simple-to-fix recipe keeps intact the ingredients' fresh flavors and crisp textures.

- 2 to 3 tablespoons oil
- 3 tablespoons chopped fresh chives or scallions
- 1 teaspoon finely chopped garlic
- 2 teaspoons chopped fresh ginger
- 1 pound sliced sugar snap or snow peas, stems and tips removed (strings pulled from sugar snaps)
- ¾ pound yellow squash, thinly sliced
- 1 red bell pepper, chopped
- 2 tablespoons freshly chopped parsley or 1 tablespoon chopped cilantro
- salt and pepper to taste

Heat oil in a wok or deep skillet. Sauté chives (or scallions), garlic and ginger until sweet-smelling—about 1 minute. Add vegetables and stir-fry until tender-crisp—about 4 or 5 minutes. Add salt and pepper to taste. Sprinkle with parsley (or cilantro) and serve.

Serves 6 to 8.

Garlicky Snowpeas Sauté ✔

Crunchy and slightly Oriental tasting, this simple combination makes the peas really shine.

- 2 tablespoons oil
- 2 or 3 cloves garlic, depending on your taste, finely chopped
- 4 scallions, chopped
- 1 large sweet red yellow or green pepper, diced or chopped
- 1 pound fresh snowpeas, trimmed
- ½ cup jicama or water chestnuts, cubed
- 2 teaspoons soy sauce

In a wok or deep skillet heat oil. Add garlic, scallions and sweet pepper and sauté until softened and fragrant, about one minute. Add the snowpeas and jicama and sauté until cooked but still very tender-crisp, 2 to 3 minutes. Add soy sauce and toss together. Taste for seasoning, adding more soy sauce if desired.

Serves 4 to 6.

INDONESIAN PILAF ✓

A quickly made and evocative main dish. Part of the fun is to serve it with little bowls of as many of the different condiments as you have on hand.

PEANUT SAUCE:
⅓ cup creamy peanut butter
1 tablespoon dry sherry
2 tablespoons rice vinegar
2 teaspoons freshly grated ginger
⅛ teaspoon cayenne pepper
½ teaspoon sugar
1 clove garlic, finely chopped
2 scallions, white part only,
  finely chopped (save tops)

RICE MIXTURE:
2 cups water
1 cup long grain white rice
2½ cups fresh peas (about 2
  pounds unshelled)
2 cups cooked chicken, cubed
½ cup chicken broth

GARNISH:
⅓ cup toasted chopped peanuts
  and reserved scallion tops

CONDIMENTS:
small bowls of chutney, sliced
  banana, raisins, coconut,
  cilantro, chopped orange,
  chopped apples, yogurt

In a saucepan, blend and stir together sauce ingredients, heating gently. Cover and keep warm. Boil water, add rice, cover tightly and reduce heat to a simmer for 15 minutes. Uncover and pour peas on top of rice, cover and simmer for another 5 minutes or until water is absorbed and rice and peas are tender. Mix in chicken. Transfer to a warm serving bowl. Toss rice mixture and chicken broth and reheated peanut sauce together. Top with peanuts and reserved chopped scallion tops. Serve with condiments.

Serves 6.

CURRIED FRESH PEA SOUP ✓

This smooth soup has a delicate, mild flavor that makes it a satisfying light lunch or supper completed with a green salad and fresh crispy bread.

3 tablespoons butter
2 cloves garlic, minced
2 onions, cut into ¼-inch slices
2 stalks celery, cut into ¼-inch
  slices
2 medium potatoes, cut into
  ¼-inch slices
1 carrot, cut into ⅛-inch slices
2½ cups fresh shelled peas
¼ teaspoon sugar
2 teaspoons curry powder
3 to 4 cups chicken broth
2 cups half-and-half or milk
salt and pepper to taste

GARNISH:
crisp bacon, finely chopped
chopped chives

In a saucepan melt butter, add garlic, onion, celery, potatoes and carrots, and sauté until softened. Add peas, sugar, curry, and 2 cups of the chicken broth. Cover and simmer 15 to 20 minutes until vegetables are very tender.

Purée mixture in blender one batch at a time. Pour back into pot; add remaining chicken broth and enough milk or half-and-half to give the desired consistency. Heat through gently at low heat; do not boil. Taste for seasoning, adding salt and pepper as needed. Garnish each bowl with crispy chopped bacon. The soup can be served either hot or cold.

Serves 6 to 8.

Peppers & Chile Peppers

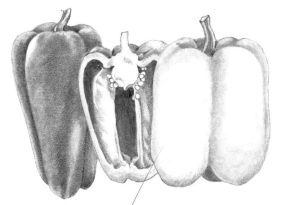

Sweet Red or Yellow Pepper Essence

Spoon this lovely sauce alongside green pesto sauce for a beautiful presentation.

**Red or yellow peppers, char/
roasted, seeded and peeled,
enough to make 2 cups pepper
chunks
½ cup pine nuts
2 cloves garlic
½ cup olive oil
½ teaspoon salt
juice of one lemon**

In food processor or blender, grind
pine nuts and garlic to a paste, then
add peppers, oil, salt and lemon
juice. Process until smooth. Use
as a condiment with broiled chicken
or fish, or cooked or raw sliced
vegetables.

Makes about 2½ cups.

Country Style Peppers & Potatoes

**4 to 5 tablespoons oil
1 medium onion, sliced very thin
1 clove garlic, finely chopped
4 medium to large boiling
potatoes, cut into paper-thin
slices
2 red bell peppers, char/roasted,
peeled, seeded and diced into
1-inch pieces
2 green bell peppers, roasted,
peeled, seeded and diced into
1-inch pieces
2 tablespoons wine vinegar
2 tablespoons fresh basil, chopped
2 teaspoons fresh tarragon, finely
chopped
½ teaspoon salt
¼ teaspoon freshly ground
pepper**

In a large heavy skillet, heat 4 tablespoons of oil. Add the onion, garlic
and potato slices and sauté over low
heat until fork-tender and lightly
browned on both sides (add more oil
if necessary). Add peppers, vinegar,
the fresh herbs, salt and pepper and
toss together for several minutes.
Taste for seasoning.

Serves 4 to 6.

MIMI'S MEXICAN CHICKEN SOUP

This delicious, colorful soup with its clean citrusy flavor will especially please cilantro aficionados!

1 tablespoon vegetable or olive oil
1 onion, chopped
2 cloves garlic, finely chopped
1 large red bell pepper, diced
1 quart homemade chicken broth
1/3 cup fresh lime juice (most authentic and best) or 1/4 cup lemon juice
1 boneless cooked chicken breast, shredded
1 cup cooked rice
1 cup chopped tomatoes
1/2 cup chopped fresh cilantro
salt and pepper to taste

GARNISH:
chopped fresh cilantro

In a large saucepan heat oil and sauté onion, garlic and bell pepper until softened and fragrant—several minutes. Add the chicken broth and bring to a boil. Add the fresh lime or lemon juice, chicken meat and rice and bring back to a boil. Add tomatoes and cilantro, then turn off heat immediately. Taste and add salt and pepper if desired. Serve immediately with cilantro sprinkled over top as a garnish to each bowl.

Serves 4 to 6.

TEX-MEX CHILE SLAW

A new version of an old favorite for spicy food lovers.

DRESSING:
Combine and shake together:
1/2 jalapeño or serrano or other fresh hot chile
1 clove finely chopped garlic
2 tablespoons wine vinegar
1 teaspoon sugar
1 teaspoon ground cumin
3 teaspoons chopped fresh oregano or 1/2 teaspoon dried
4 tablespoons olive oil
1/4 teaspoon salt
generous pinch of cayenne pepper

SLAW:
2 bell peppers seeded and cut into thin strips (use several colors if possible)
1 Anaheim or other mild chile, cut into very thin strips
1 small red onion cut in half then into very fine strips
2 carrots cut into very thin sticks, about as long as the pepper strips
1/2 head of cabbage, finely cut or coarsely shredded
optional garnish: 1 tablespoon chopped cilantro

Prepare dressing. Combine the vegetables in a salad bowl and toss with the dressing. Let marinate at least 1/2 hour before serving. Garnish with cilantro.

Serves 4 to 6.

Chicken Santa Cruz

The aromatic, subtle flavors of this dish have drawn more raves than many other entrées we've prepared. Slow sautéing brings out the sweetness of the spices, herbs and onions and the rich mellow flavor of ripe peppers. Please do try it. Don't forget crusty French bread. By the way, leftovers make great sandwiches.

4 portions boneless chicken breast, skinned and cut into ½-inch strips

2 tablespoons lemon juice

4 large fresh bell peppers—use red, yellow, purple or deep green peppers (or any combination)

4 tablespoons salad oil or very light olive oil

2 cloves garlic, finely chopped

2 large onions, finely sliced

1 teaspoon whole or ½ teaspoon ground cumin seed

1½ teaspoons fresh or 1 teaspoon dried oregano

1½ teaspoons finely chopped fresh hot chile pepper or ½ teaspoon dried hot pepper flakes

½ teaspoon salt (or to taste)

¼ teaspoon freshly ground pepper

2 tablespoons finely chopped fresh parsley or 1 tablespoon chopped cilantro

Sprinkle chicken strips with lemon juice and set aside. Cut peppers in half and remove seeds and ribs. Cut into 1½-inch-wide strips. In a large skillet, heat the oil. Add garlic and cook one minute on moderate heat. Add the pepper strips, sliced onion, cumin, oregano and chile pepper. Stir the vegetables to coat evenly with oil. Cover and cook over medium heat for 10 minutes. Uncover pan, stir mixture, add chicken strips and stir to distribute them evenly in the vegetable mixture. Cover skillet again and cook gently for 10 more minutes. Uncover; chicken should be cooked through and vegetable mixture should be tender and very aromatic. Add salt and pepper to taste. Sprinkle with chopped parsley or cilantro and serve.

Serves 4 to 6.

CORRALITOS RICE CASSEROLE

A local favorite influenced by our on-going love affair with Tex-Mex cuisine. Great for potlucks and big gatherings and generally loved by everyone who has some!

3 cups cooked rice
2 cups "light" sour cream
5 scallions, chopped
salt and pepper to taste
1½ cups cooked corn kernels—about two ears
3 coarsely chopped, mild green Anaheim or Poblano chiles, char/roasted, peeled and seeded. Makes about ⅔ cup, (or use two four-ounce cans of "California" mild green chiles)
1½ cups shredded Jack cheese
⅓ cup shredded Cheddar cheese

GARNISH:
2 tablespoons chopped fresh cilantro

Preheat oven to 350°.

Mix the rice with the sour cream and scallions and add salt and pepper to taste. Spread half of the rice mixture in the bottom of a greased 1½-quart casserole; top with half of the corn, half of the chiles, and half of the Jack cheese. Repeat with the rest of the rice mixture, then the rest of the corn, chiles and Jack cheese. Top with the Cheddar cheese.

Bake covered for 20 minutes, then uncover for 10 minutes to finish. Sprinkle with cilantro. Serve hot or warm.

Serves 6 to 8.

CRAB-STUFFED CHILE RELLENOS

Low in calories; rich in flavor.

8 Anaheim chiles

FILLING:
½ pound cooked crab or Surimi mock crabmeat
2 teaspoons fresh lemon juice
1 teaspoon hot mustard or 1½ teaspoons Dijon mustard
2 egg whites, lightly beaten
2 tablespoons finely chopped fresh basil
¾ cup fresh bread crumbs

Preheat oven to 375°.

Prepare chiles by char/roasting on an asador or under broiler. Place in plastic bag to cool for 10 minutes. Peel the chiles under cold water. Slice open one side and remove seeds.

Sprinkle crab with lemon juice. Stir in mustard, mixing well. Add egg whites and basil and blend. Add bread crumbs and toss mixture together. Open chiles flat and fill with filling, then fold chiles together. Place stuffed chiles on greased baking sheet, cover tightly with foil and bake for 20 minutes.

Serves 4 to 6.

STUFFED PEPPERS SANTA CRUZ STYLE ✔

An updated and delicious version of down-home comfort food that will please all comers!
Use several colors of peppers for best effect.

4 large green, red or yellow bell
  peppers
3 cups chicken stock
1 cup long grain rice
2 mild Italian sausages, casings
  removed
2 tablespoons olive oil
1 onion, chopped
½ red bell pepper, chopped
1 Anaheim chile pepper, char/
  roasted, peeled, seeded and
  chopped, or use 1 canned "California" mild green chile
½ teaspoon celery seed
2 tablespoons lemon juice
½ cup chopped cilantro
salt and pepper to taste
Parmesan cheese
optional but delicious to add:
  ¼ cup chopped sun-dried
  tomatoes

Preheat oven to 350°.

Cut off the tops of the bell peppers and remove core and seeds. Cook in boiling salted water for 3 minutes to blanch. Remove from pan and turn upside-down to drain. Bring 2½ cups of the chicken stock to a boil (reserving remaining ½ cup) add rice, cover tightly and simmer for 20 minutes without removing the lid. In a large skillet break up the sausage into small pieces. Sauté until lightly browned. Remove sausage and place on paper towels to drain. Heat olive oil in skillet, add onion, red pepper (and sun-dried tomatoes if used) and sauté until onion is translucent. Stir in rice, sausage, chile pepper, celery seed, lemon juice, cilantro, and reserved ½ cup chicken stock. Cook until thoroughly heated and liquid is absorbed. Add salt and pepper to taste. Stuff peppers with rice mixture. Arrange them side by side in a baking dish. Sprinkle tops with Parmesan cheese. Pour ½ cup boiling water around the peppers. Bake at 350° for 30 to 35 minutes.

Serves 4.

HOMEMADE CREOLE SAUCE
WITH CHICKEN OR SHRIMP

The ingredients of homemade Creole sauce go together quickly and its rich full flavor is unbeatable when prepared with fresh ingredients.

1 tablespoon butter or margarine
3 tablespoons vegetable oil
¼ cup flour
1 large onion, coarsely chopped
2 stalks celery cut into ½-inch slices
1 red bell pepper cut into ½-inch dice
2 cloves garlic, minced
2½ pounds fresh tomatoes, peeled and coarsely chopped (about 5 cups), including juice
1 eight-ounce can tomato sauce
1 teaspoon fresh thyme or ½ teaspoon dried
1 small bay leaf
½ teaspoon black pepper
pinch of red pepper flakes
¼ teaspoon Tabasco sauce
1 teaspoon brown sugar
1½ cups chicken broth
salt and cayenne pepper
hot rice to serve with creole
2 pounds peeled, deveined raw shrimp or 4 skinned and boned chicken breasts cut in small chunks

GARNISH:
chopped parsley

In a large dutch oven, stock pot or skillet, heat butter and 1 tablespoon of the oil; add flour and stir with a wooden spoon until flour turns golden brown. Remove the flour mixture from the pot and set aside. Heat 2 more tablespoons oil in the pot and add onion, celery, peppers and garlic. Sauté for about 3 to 5 minutes until softened. Add the reserved flour mixture and all the remaining ingredients except salt and cayenne. Bring to a boil. Reduce heat, cover and simmer for 30 to 40 minutes until thickened. Season with the salt and cayenne to taste. Remove the bay leaf.

Just before serving, heat sauce to a simmer. If using shrimp: add raw shrimp and cook for 2 to 3 minutes, just until shrimp turn pink. If using chicken: add chicken chunks and cook 3 to 5 minutes or until done. You can also use a half-chicken and half-shrimp combination.

Serve hot creole over hot cooked rice. Garnish with chopped parsley.

Makes 6 cups sauce; serves 6.

CHICKEN FAJITAS

A juicy, mildly spicy light chicken dish that uses lots of fresh colorful sweet peppers. Quick and easy to make, we know it will bring requests for second and even third helpings!

3 **Anaheim or Poblano chiles, charred, seeded and cut into strips, or 3 tablespoons chopped canned mild chiles**
2 **medium tomatoes, seeded and chopped**
1 **tablespoon fresh oregano, finely chopped, or 2 teaspoons dried**
1 **teaspoon ground cumin**
2 **teaspoons good quality chile powder**
½ **teaspoon salt**
2 **tablespoons flour**
1 **pound skinned and boned chicken breasts cut into ½-inch strips**
4 **tablespoons oil**
1 **large onion, thinly sliced**
2 **small cloves garlic, finely chopped**
3 **large bell peppers, yellow, red and green (or at least 2 colors), thinly sliced**
optional: 1 tablespoon fresh cilantro, chopped
to serve: warmed flour tortillas, sour cream, tomato salsa

Combine the chiles, tomatoes, oregano, cumin, chile powder, salt and flour with the chicken strips and mix together well. Set aside to marinate briefly.

Heat 2 tablespoons of the oil in a large deep skillet and sauté the onion and garlic until softened, 3 to 4 minutes. Add the bell pepper strips and sauté about 5 minutes more, until the peppers are slightly softened and cooked, but still crisp. Remove from skillet and keep warm.

Heat the remaining 2 tablespoons of oil in the skillet. Sauté the marinated chicken strips, stirring and tossing until strips are cooked through and lose their pink color when sliced. Add the sautéed pepper mixture and heat and mix together with chicken. Stir in cilantro if used.

Serve the fajitas mixture spooned onto warm flour tortillas and pass sour cream and salsa as condiments. Each diner folds his or her tortilla over the fajita mixture to enjoy. Have extra tortillas handy.

Serves 4 to 6.

POTATOES

DILLY POTATO SALAD

*Peas and potatoes in a creamy dressing
with the bright flavor note of fresh dill.*

1½ pounds new potatoes, steamed
   and cut into chunks
1 cup cooked peas, drained
½ cup chopped celery

DRESSING:
¼ teaspoon salt
1 clove garlic, halved
2 tablespoons white wine vinegar
1 tablespoon Dijon mustard
½ teaspoon sugar
¼ cup mayonnaise
½ cup plain yogurt
6 scallions, finely sliced
6 tablespoons chopped fresh dill
freshly ground pepper

GARNISH:
sprigs of fresh dill

Prepare potatoes and peas and combine with celery. Set aside. Sprinkle
salt in a pretty salad bowl. Rub
garlic around bowl—discard garlic.
Add vinegar, mustard, sugar, mayonnaise, yogurt, scallions and dill. Mix
until combined. Add potatoes, peas
and celery and freshly ground pepper
to taste and mix together gently.
Garnish with sprigs of dill.

Serves 6 to 8.

ROASTED POTATOES WITH GARLIC AND HERBS

*The aromas of roasting potatoes, herbs
and garlic make this an irresistible dish.*

3 tablespoons olive oil
1 dozen small or 6 medium
   potatoes, washed but not
   peeled, cut in ½-inch slices
   and patted dry
½ to 1 head of garlic, separated
   into cloves and peeled, or to
   taste
4 or 5 sprigs, 4 to 6 inches long,
   of rosemary, thyme or basil—
   your choice

Preheat oven to 400°.
   Spread olive oil in bottom of a
9 × 13-inch glass baking dish. Toss
potato slices and garlic cloves in
baking dish to coat with oil, then
arrange into a single layer. Lay the
sprigs of herbs on top of the potatoes. Cover the pan with foil or a
cookie sheet and bake 20 minutes.
Uncover and bake 15 to 20 minutes
more or until potatoes are tender
and begin to brown. Carefully remove herbs and discard. Serve
immediately.

Serves 4.

RADISHES

RADISH AND CUCUMBER SALAD

Combines two crunchy vegetables in an herb-scented sweet-and-sour dressing.

- ¾ cup cider vinegar
- ¼ cup sugar
- 3 tablespoons chopped fresh dill
- 2 tablespoons chopped fresh parsley
- ¾ teaspoon mustard seed
- ¼ teaspoon salt and pepper
- 3 large cucumbers, scored and very thinly sliced
- 1 cup thinly sliced radishes

Combine vinegar, sugar, dill, parsley, mustard seed and salt and pepper; stir to dissolve sugar. Add cucumbers and let marinate in refrigerator for several hours. To serve: add the radishes and mix thoroughly.

Serves 6.

CRUNCHY RADISHES WITH CREAMY SESAME DRESSING

This sesame dressing sets off the flavor of crispy radishes in a new and exotic fashion.

- 1½ cups of radishes, thinly sliced
- 1 three-fourths-inch length of daikon radish (if available), thinly sliced to matchstick size
- ¼ cup of roasted sesame tahini (sesame paste available at health and specialty food stores)
- 5 scallions sliced thin, including part of the green leaves
- 3 tablespoons dry sherry
- 2 tablespoons lemon juice
- ¼ teaspoon each salt and sugar
- ¼ cup water
- optional: ⅓ cup chopped or sliced almonds
- 1 cup cooked cubed chicken meat

Combine radishes in a bowl. For the dressing, stir the rest of the ingredients into the tahini; it will be a thick paste. Thin dressing to a creamy consistency with the water. Combine radishes with dressing and toss. Taste for seasoning. Sprinkle with chopped nuts if desired. Serve on lettuce. For a main-dish salad, mix in 1 cup cooked cubed chicken meat with the almonds.

Serves 4.

SALADS & SALAD DRESSINGS

SPICY THAI VINAIGRETTE

Wonderful over crunchy lettuces.

> 1 small clove finely chopped
>   garlic
> ¼ teaspoon finely chopped fresh
>   ginger
> 3 tablespoons rice vinegar
> 1 teaspoon brown sugar
> 1 teaspoon soy sauce
> ¼ cup vegetable oil
> ½ teaspoon sesame oil
> ¼ teaspoon red pepper flakes or
>   chile oil
> optional: chopped red onions or
>   mandarin oranges; sliced
>   jicama

Combine all ingredients and mix
well. Pour over mixed lettuces, toss
and serve.

Serves 4 to 6.

LEMON BASIL
PESTO DRESSING

Especially for lemon lovers.

> ⅓ cup lemon basil leaves
> 1 small clove garlic, chopped
> ½ teaspoon fresh oregano, finely
>   chopped, or ¼ teaspoon dried
> 3 tablespoons olive oil
> 2 tablespoons salad oil
> 1½ tablespoons fresh lemon juice
> ¼ cup freshly grated Parmesan
>   cheese
> freshly ground pepper
> optional: ¼ cup pine nuts

Combine ingredients in blender and
blend briefly to emulsify. Serve over
fresh lettuce.

Serves 2.

3-GREEN SALAD DRESSING

Healthy, delicious, and quickly made in a blender.

> 1 cup (tightly packed) spinach
>   leaves
> ¾ cup loosely packed parsley
>   leaves
> 3 tablespoons chopped fresh basil
> 3 tablespoons lemon juice
> ¼ cup herb or cider vinegar
> ½ teaspoon salt
> ½ teaspoon freshly ground
>   pepper
> ½ teaspoon ground cumin
> 1 small clove garlic, finely
>   chopped
> ½ cup olive oil

Combine all ingredients in blender and blend until smooth. Use over any of your favorite fresh green salads. This tasty dressing can be stored in a covered container in the refrigerator for 2 to 3 weeks for later use.

Makes about 3 cups.

CREAMY RASPBERRY DRESSING

Elegant and rich-tasting, this dressing is very special with soft-leaved lettuces.

> 3 tablespoons Shepherd's Perseus
>   Raspberry Vinegar
> 1 tablespoon sugar
> ⅓ cup light olive oil
> 1 tablespoon sour cream
> 1 tablespoon Dijon mustard
> ½ cup fresh or frozen and
>   defrosted raspberries
> ½ cup toasted walnuts
> 2 heads fresh bibb or butterhead
>   lettuce, washed and torn

Whisk together the vinegar, sugar, oil, cream, mustard and about half the berries. Put lettuce in salad bowl or on plates and top with nuts and reserved berries. Drizzle with whisked dressing and serve.

Serves 4 to 6.

Fresh Orange Salad Dressing

The fresh orange flavor comes through in this light and refreshing dressing that really makes salad greens sing.

- ¼ cup mild vinegar
- 1 teaspoon freshly grated orange rind
- ⅓ cup freshly squeezed orange juice
- 1 tablespoon minced parsley
- 1 teaspoon sugar
- ¼ teaspoon Worcestershire sauce
- ¼ teaspoon salt
- ½ teaspoon paprika
- ½ cup salad oil

Combine ingredients and blend or shake together thoroughly.

Makes 1¼ cups.

Sweet and Sour Roquefort Dressing

Perfect for big wedges of lettuce or assorted mixed greens.

- ⅓ cup olive oil
- ¼ teaspoon paprika
- ½ teaspoon dry mustard
- ½ teaspoon sugar
- 1 tablespoon herb vinegar
- 1 tablespoon lemon juice
- 1 tablespoon dry white wine
- 1 teaspoon Worcestershire sauce
- 2 tablespoons Roquefort cheese, crumbled
- freshly grated pepper to taste.

Combine ingredients and blend. Serve over lettuces and/or mixed greens.

Dresses a salad for 4.

Shepherd's Salad Dressing

Fine-quality ingredients turn this classically simple vinaigrette into the perfect complement for all fresh salads.

- ½ cup Shepherd's Ponente Extra Virgin Olive Oil (or another top quality light olive oil)
- ¼ cup Shepherd's Perseus Raspberry Vinegar (or another very fruity and not too tart raspberry vinegar)
- ½ teaspon Dijon-style mustard
- ¼ teaspoon salt
- ½ to 1 clove fresh garlic, as you like

Combine all ingredients and shake to blend in a glass jar or whisk together thoroughly by hand. Before using, remove garlic clove.

Dresses a salad for 6 to 8.

Tarragon Ginger Dressing

This is a piquant, almost spicy dressing that is equally good used hot over greens or at room temperature over mixed lettuces.

- 1 tablespoon vegetable oil
- 1 small clove garlic, minced
- 2 tablespoons finely chopped scallion
- ½ cup chicken broth
- 2 tablespoons red wine vinegar
- 1 teaspoon finely grated ginger
- 2 tablespoons chopped fresh tarragon or 1 teaspoon dried
- 2 tablespoons olive oil
- salt and freshly ground pepper to taste

In a skillet, heat oil. Add garlic and scallion and sauté until softened. Add broth and boil until the liquid is reduced by half—about 3 or 4 minutes. Stir in vinegar and cook an additional 2 minutes. Transfer to a bowl. Add ginger and tarragon. Gradually whisk in the olive oil. Add salt and pepper to taste.

Dresses a salad for 4 to 6.

Sesame Salad Dressing

The flavor of nutty sesame underscores this unusual and delicious dressing for mixed greens.

- 1 clove garlic, finely chopped
- 2 tablespoons tahini (sesame seed paste)
- 1 teaspoon honey
- ¼ cup lemon juice
- ¾ teaspoon ground cumin
- ½ cup olive oil
- 2 tablespoons freshly chopped parsley
- ¼ teaspoon salt
- freshly ground pepper

Mix all ingredients together in a blender and process until well combined. Taste for seasoning, adding more salt to taste. Serve over mixed salad greens.

Makes about 1 cup dressing.

ROMAINE SALAD WITH FETA DRESSING

The sweet crunchy leaves of romaine go especially well with the slight tang of feta cheese.

2 tablespoons red wine vinegar
1 tablespoon white wine
2 ounces feta cheese
  (5 tablespoons)
¼ cup olive oil
salt and freshly ground pepper
1 head romaine lettuce, rinsed,
  dried and torn for salad
1 small cucumber, seeded and
  chopped
2 tablespoons parsley, finely
  chopped

In a bowl combine vinegar, wine and cheese, and add the oil in a thin stream, whisking until it is blended. Add salt and pepper to taste. Combine lettuce and cucumber and toss with dressing. Sprinkle with parsley before serving.

Serves 4.

BUTTERMILK BLUE CHEESE DRESSING

Buttermilk dressing low in fat, piquant and flavorful.

½ cup fresh buttermilk
¼ cup crumbled blue cheese
1 tablespoon olive oil
1 finely chopped scallion
2 tablespoons red wine vinegar
2 tablespoons finely chopped
  parsley
pinch of sugar
salt and pepper to taste

Combine all ingredients and blend. Pour over mixed salad greens, toss and serve.

Dresses a salad for 6.

ROASTED GARLIC DRESSING

This dressing is delicious with any green salad and will make your salad course a real event. Roasting the garlic gives it a wonderfully mellow and sweet mild flavor.

5 or 6 fat cloves of garlic,
  unpeeled
¼ cup olive oil
2 medium tomatoes, chopped
  and drained
2 tablespoons freshly squeezed
  lemon juice
3 chopped scallions, white part
  only
2 tablespoons any herb vinegar
  or use wine vinegar
⅓ cup finely chopped fresh basil

Heat oven to 350°.

Brush the garlic cloves well with 1 teaspoon of the oil, reserving the remaining oil. Roast the oiled garlic cloves in a pan until golden and soft—about 10–15 minutes. Watch carefully so garlic does not get over-brown. Remove and cool. When cool enough to handle, peel the garlic and combine the pulp with the reserved oil and rest of the ingredients in a blender. Blend until smooth and use to dress any mixed green salad.

Makes about 1 cup.

CRUNCHY RED AND GREEN SALAD

Lots of flavor and texture in this serious salad that really rewards your mouth.

DRESSING:
1 scallion, finely chopped
½ teaspoon fresh thyme, finely chopped
1 tablespoon fresh parsley, finely chopped
1 teaspoon Dijon mustard
2 tablespoons white vinegar
1 tablespoon white wine
¼ cup light olive oil

SALAD INGREDIENTS:
½ to 1 head radicchio, broken into mixed salad-sized pieces. Use less if you don't like its tartness; more if you do.
2 heads of young and tender curly endive, washed, dried, and torn into pieces
1 large green-skinned apple (Granny Smiths or Pippins are best), cut into ¼-inch slices

Combine dressing ingredients and mix well. In a large salad bowl, combine salad ingredients. Whisk dressing again and pour over salad. Toss and serve.

Serves 4.

ISLAND SIN SALAD ✓

Wickedly delicious.

DRESSING:
3 tablespoons lemon juice
2 tablespoons honey
4 teaspoons soy sauce
1½ teaspoons *freshly* grated ginger
1 small clove of garlic, finely chopped
large pinch of white pepper
½ cup light vegetable oil

SALAD INGREDIENTS:
2 small heads of lettuce, washed and torn into serving-size pieces
1 large peeled orange, cut into segments, or one can drained mandarin oranges
¼ cup sunflower seeds, toasted optional (but very good): ¼ cup chopped cilantro

Combine dressing ingredients, whisking oil in thoroughly. Put lettuce in salad bowl, add cilantro if used, and arrange orange slices over the lettuce. Sprinkle the salad with the sunflower seeds. Whisk the dressing again to be sure it is well combined. Pour over salad, toss and serve.

Serves 4 to 6.

ARUGULA AND NECTARINE SALAD

Green tangy arugula contrasts with luscious fresh nectarine slices all set off by a delicate raspberry vinaigrette. A beautiful presentation and great flavor. You can substitute fresh pears or peaches if nectarines aren't available.

DRESSING:
3 tablespoons Shepherd's Perseus Raspberry Vinegar (or another very fruity and not too tart raspberry vinegar)
1 teaspoon Dijon mustard
5 tablespoons olive or vegetable oil
pinch each of sugar, salt and pepper

SALAD INGREDIENTS:
4 cups torn arugula leaves
4 cups torn butter lettuce leaves
2 or 3 ripe nectarines, cut into slices
⅓ cup toasted walnuts (toast 5 to 8 minutes in 300° oven or toaster oven)

Combine dressing ingredients and mix together well. Arrange salad ingredients in bowl. Pour dressing over them. Sprinkle with walnuts at the table so diners can see how pretty the salad looks in its bowl.

Serves 6 to 8.

WARM SPINACH SALAD WITH ARUGULA

The slightly spicy arugula and the spinach are beautifully set off by the full-flavored mushroom dressing.

1 large bunch spinach (about 1 pound), washed, dried and torn
2 cups arugula leaves
4 tablespoons olive oil
¾ pound mushrooms, sliced
4 scallions, sliced
4 tablespoons wine vinegar
2 teaspoons sugar
salt and pepper
⅓ cup toasted pine nuts or walnuts
⅓ pound feta cheese, crumbled

Arrange spinach and arugula leaves in a salad bowl. Set aside. Heat oil in a medium skillet, add mushrooms and scallions, and sauté until softened and mushrooms have released a little liquid. Add vinegar, sugar, salt and pepper, stirring until heated through. Pour the mixture immediately over spinach and arugula. Sprinkle with nuts and feta cheese and serve.

Serves 4 to 6.

LAYERED GREEK SALAD

This cool, colorful and appetite-pleasing layered salad is definitely something to look forward to on a hot and sultry summer day.

DRESSING:
Combine all ingredients:
1 clove garlic, minced
½ teaspoon salt
2 tablespoons lemon juice
3 tablespoons wine vinegar
½ teaspoon ground cumin
½ cup olive oil
1 teaspoon chopped fresh
 oregano or ½ teaspoon dried
⅛ teaspoon freshly ground
 pepper

SEASONING MIXTURE:
Combine and mix in a small bowl:
1 bunch scallions, including tops,
 thinly sliced
½ cup fresh mint leaves, chopped
½ to ¾ cup quartered pitted
 Greek olives (to taste)
½ pound feta cheese, crumbled

SALAD INGREDIENTS:
2 large cucumbers, peeled and
 cut into ½-inch dice
1 red bell pepper, seeded and cut
 into ½-inch dice
1 green, yellow or orange bell
 pepper seeded and cut into
 ½-inch dice
4 large tomatoes, seeded and cut
 into ½-inch dice, well drained

GARNISH:
chopped fresh parsley

In a deep large glass serving bowl, alternate a layer of each chopped raw vegetable with the seasoning mixture, beginning with the cucumbers, then peppers, and finally the tomatoes, so that each vegetable has a layer of the seasoning mixture between it and the next vegetable. Whisk the dressing and pour it evenly over the salad. Garnish with chopped parsley and then refrigerate the salad for at least ½ hour to let the flavors blend. You can prepare this salad up to 8 hours ahead.

Serves 4 to 6.

Spinach

Baked Spinach Gnocchi

An easy-to-make version of this classic Italian delicacy.

1 very large bunch of spinach
1 cup low-fat ricotta cheese
1 cup freshly grated Parmesan or
   Asiago cheese
2 tablespoons chopped parsley
1 chopped scallion
1 tablespoon lemon juice
1 egg yolk
2 tablespoons flour
½ teaspoon freshly grated
   nutmeg
¼ teaspoon salt
¼ teaspoon white pepper
extra flour for shaping gnocchi
1 cup shredded Mozzarella cheese

Preheat oven to 350°.

Steam or cook spinach briefly until tender. Drain well and chop fine. You should have 1 generous cup. Thoroughly combine spinach, ricotta cheese, Parmesan, parsley, scallion, lemon juice, egg yolk, flour, nutmeg, salt and pepper. Shape the mixture into little logs about 2 inches long and 1 inch in diameter. If sticky, sprinkle them lightly with additional flour. Place on a wax-paper-lined baking sheet.

Cook the gnocchi in batches by carefully dropping them a few at a time into a large pot of gently boiling water. When they are cooked they will rise to the top—this just takes several minutes. Transfer them with a slotted spoon to a greased baking dish, laying them side by side in a single layer. Sprinkle the Mozzarella cheese over the top. Bake 10 minutes or until well heated through and lightly browned.

Serves 2 or 3 as a main course or 4 to 6 as first course.

CRUSTLESS SPINACH PIE ✓

The spinach mixture forms a crust of its own with a pizza-like filling that will please everyone.

2 pounds fresh spinach, stalks
  removed
salt
2 teaspoons lemon juice
3 tablespoons sour cream
1 tablespoon butter
2 scallions, chopped
½ pound fresh sliced mushrooms
4 tomatoes, diced and well-
  drained
1 large clove garlic, minced
1 tablespoon fresh thyme or
  1 teaspoon dried
2 tablespoons minced parsley
salt and pepper
2 to 3 tablespoons Parmesan
  cheese, freshly grated
1 tablespoon butter

Preheat oven to 400°.

Wash spinach thoroughly. Without shaking the water off the leaves, place into a large pot over high heat. As the spinach steams, sprinkle with salt and mash the leaves with a wooden spoon. After 2 or 3 minutes, turn off the heat and leave until cool enough to handle. Take handfuls of spinach and squeeze out as much water as possible. Chop coarsely. Place in a bowl; sprinkle with lemon juice and mix in sour cream.

In a saucepan, melt butter, sauté scallions until soft, add mushrooms and sauté for 3 to 5 minutes. Add tomatoes and turn up heat, stirring so that the liquid cooks away. Add garlic, thyme and parsley and simmer 2 or 3 minutes longer.

Grease an 8- or 9-inch Pyrex pie plate. Spread part of the spinach over the bottom and the remaining portion up the sides as if forming a pie shell. In the center spoon the mushroom-tomato mixture. Sprinkle with salt, pepper and Parmesan cheese. Dot with butter. Bake 15 minutes. Serve in wedges, hot or at room temperature.

Makes 4 to 6 servings.

Squash & Pumpkins

Indonesian Zucchini Salad/Pickle

Serve with grilled meats and/or chicken as a salad or relish.

1 pound zucchini (about 5 medium), cut into matchstick strips
1½ cups shredded cabbage
1 carrot, coarsely grated
1 tablespoon salt
1 onion, finely chopped
1 large clove garlic, finely chopped
1 tablespoon finely chopped fresh ginger
2 tablespoons finely chopped peanuts or almonds
2 tablespoons vegetable oil
¼ teaspoon red pepper flakes
½ teaspoon ground turmeric
½ cup rice vinegar
1 tablespoon firmly packed brown sugar

GARNISH:
chopped peanuts and chopped cilantro or parsley

Sprinkle zucchini, cabbage and carrot with salt. Let stand several hours. Rinse in cold water; drain and pat dry and set aside. Combine the onions, garlic, ginger and peanuts and set aside.

In a large heavy skillet, heat oil, then add the onion mixture, pepper flakes and turmeric. Cook over moderately low heat, stirring frequently, for 5 to 8 minutes. Stir in vinegar and sugar and cook an additional 3 to 5 minutes or until slightly thickened. Add the drained zucchini, cabbage and carrot, stirring until coated with the mixture. Cool to room temperature. Chill for at least 2 hours before serving. Will keep covered in refrigerator for several weeks. Just before serving garnish with peanuts and cilantro or parsley.

Makes about 4 cups.

SUMMER SQUASH CHOWDER ✔

A new combination of flavors enhances this light clam chowder.

2 tablespoons oil or butter
1 large onion, chopped
1 cup celery, chopped
4 or 5 medium-sized yellow summer squash, sliced into 1-inch pieces
1 medium potato, cut into small cubes
1 tablespoon flour
3 cups chicken broth
2 six-and-one-half-ounce cans of chopped clams and their juice
1 ear of corn cut from cob or ¾ cup frozen corn
1 teaspoon fresh thyme or ½ teaspoon dried
⅛ teaspoon Tabasco sauce
1 tablespoon fresh parsley, finely chopped
1 cup milk (low-fat or regular, not skim)
1 cup grated Cheddar cheese

Heat oil or butter in large saucepan. Add onion, celery, squash and potato and sauté for five minutes. Remove from heat. Sprinkle with the flour, stirring to coat vegetables. Add the chicken broth, bring to a boil and then lower heat and simmer covered for about 15 minutes or until vegetables are tender. Add the 2 cans of clams and their juice, the corn, thyme, Tabasco sauce, and parsley. Return to a boil for 2 to 3 minutes. Reduce heat to a simmer. Add milk and cheese and heat through but do not boil. Stir well and serve piping hot.

Serves 4 to 6.

GRILLED ZUCCHINI WITH FRESH ROSEMARY BUTTER ✔

Delicious with squash, this tasty herb butter also goes perfectly with corn or green beans and is a tasty alternative to garlic butter on toasted French bread loaves. It freezes well too.

ROSEMARY BUTTER:
2 scallions, white part only, finely chopped
2 tablespoons finely chopped fresh rosemary leaves
¼ teaspoon fresh ground pepper
1 teaspoon lemon juice
½ teaspoon finely grated lemon rind
pinch ground cayenne pepper
¼ pound (1 stick) salted butter, at room temperature

GRILLED ZUCCHINI:
6 medium zucchini
olive oil

Thoroughly blend together the rosemary butter ingredients, then transfer to a deep custard cup or butter server, or place on a 12-inch-long piece of plastic wrap and roll into a 1-inch-thick log. Chill the herbed butter slightly to firm and let flavors blend.

Slice zucchini lengthwise into thirds so you have long slices about ½ inch thick. Brush with olive oil. Grill or broil them until cooked and soft inside. Top each zucchini slice with a portion of the rosemary butter and serve.

Serves 3 to 4.

VICKI SEBASTIANI'S RICOTTA-STUFFED SQUASH BLOSSOMS

This recipe appeared in our first cookbook too, but it is so often requested we decided to reprint it here for anyone who may have missed it.

12 to 15 fresh squash blossoms; number used will vary depending on size, so have a few extra on hand.

FILLING:
1 pound ricotta cheese
1 medium onion, very finely chopped
½ cup toasted almonds, finely chopped
½ cup freshly grated Italian Asiago (or Parmesan) cheese
½ teaspoon ground pepper
1 teaspoon seasoning salt
2 tablespoons fresh, finely chopped basil
2 tablespoons finely chopped parsley
2 tablespoons melted butter

Preheat oven to 350°.
  Mix all the filling ingredients together except the melted butter. Stuff squash blossoms carefully; don't overfill. Drizzle the melted butter over blossoms and bake in 350° oven for 15 minutes.

Serves 4.

FRAN'S ZUCCHINI WITH PEANUT SAUCE

Quick and easy to make, this lavish-tasting dish will delight peanut lovers.

1 pound zucchini (about 5 medium), cut into 2- to 3-inch matchstick strips
2 teaspoons vegetable oil
1 clove garlic, finely chopped
1 teaspoon fresh ginger, very finely chopped
pinch of red pepper flakes
2 tablespoons oyster sauce
3 tablespoons rice vinegar (don't substitute because rice vinegar is very mild)
3 tablespoons chicken broth
¼ cup ground or very finely chopped peanuts
pinch sugar

In a large skillet, heat oil, add garlic, ginger and red pepper flakes, and sauté until fragrant and softened—no more than one minute. Add oyster sauce, rice vinegar, chicken broth, ground peanuts and sugar. Add zucchini sticks and sauté, stirring often, just until zucchini are tender-crisp—3 to 5 minutes. Don't overcook. Serve immediately as a hot dish, or at room temperature as a salad or take-along.

Serves 4 to 6.

FRESH ZUCCHINI RELLENOS ✓

A satisfying main dish with lots of color and flavor.

6 medium zucchini
1½ cups fresh corn kernels—(use frozen and defrosted if fresh is unavailable)
2 eggs
2 tablespoons milk
¼ teaspoon salt
½ pound grated Cheddar cheese— about 2 cups
2 tablespoons butter at room temperature
2 tablespoons chopped fresh Anaheim green mild chiles, or use chopped canned mild green "California" chiles

SAUCE:
4 large fresh tomatoes, chopped (or use 1 pound drained canned solid pack tomatoes)
⅓ cup chopped onions
2 cloves chopped garlic
¼ teaspoon salt
2 tablespoons olive oil
⅓ cup fresh chopped cilantro

In blender, combine the tomatoes, onion, garlic and salt. Heat oil in a skillet. Add tomato mixture and heat about 15 minutes until thickened. Stir in cilantro.

Serves 4 to 6.

Preheat oven to 350°.

Cut zucchini in half lengthwise. Carefully scoop out the flesh and discard or save for another use. Place the zucchini shells in a greased shallow baking pan in a single layer. Combine the corn, eggs, milk and salt in a blender and blend to a coarse purée. Add chopped chiles. Mix 1½ cups of the grated cheese into the corn mixture. (Reserve ½ cup for topping.) Fill the zucchini shells with the corn mixture. Sprinkle with the remaining cheese. Dot with butter. Cover with foil and bake until tender, approximately 30 minutes. Do not overbake. Top with the freshly cooked tomato sauce.

ZUCCHINI PANCAKES ✓

Easy to make and very low in calories, these vegetable pancakes make a fine lunch or brunch dish.

6 medium zucchini
¾ teaspoon salt
1 tablespoon lemon juice
2 scallions, finely chopped
4 tablespoons fresh finely chopped basil or 2 tablespoons dried
2 small cloves garlic, finely chopped
4 eggs, lightly beaten
2 tablespoons butter
2 tablespoons oil

Shred zucchini, sprinkle with the salt and let stand for 5 to 10 minutes to draw off moisture. Squeeze or wring the shredded zucchini in a clean kitchen towel to remove all the moisture you can. Combine the squeezed-out zucchini with the rest of the ingredients except the butter and oil, mixing well. Heat the butter and oil in a heavy skillet. Spoon the zucchini mixture into the heated skillet, shaping into pancakes. Cook over medium heat until set and light brown. Flip pancakes and finish cooking the other side.

Serve whole or cut into wedges. Sour cream or very fresh plain yogurt makes a nice accompaniment.

Serves 4.

TEN-MINUTE ZUCCHINI PIZZA

A surefire way for kids (of all ages) to enjoy zucchini.

Preheat oven to 425°.

Cut medium zucchini lengthwise into ¼-inch slices. Pat dry and brush both sides with olive oil. Arrange side by side on an aluminum-foil-lined baking sheet or pizza pan. Bake 7 minutes or until just tender when pierced with a fork. Top generously with well-seasoned pizza sauce (any bottled kind you like is fine). Sprinkle with chopped fresh basil, freshly grated Mozzarella and Parmesan cheese and put back in the oven for 2 to 3 minutes, until sauce is hot and bubbly and cheese is melted.

Serve immediately.

DRUNKEN APPLE/PUMPKIN PIE ✓

A dramatic finish adds fun to this delectable dessert.

1 unbaked 9-inch pie shell
1 cup cooked and mashed
   pumpkin or winter squash,
   well drained
1 cup thick, chunky applesauce
2 eggs
¾ cup firmly packed brown sugar
1 tablespoon flour
½ teaspoon salt
1 teaspoon cinnamon
1 teaspoon ginger
¼ teaspoon nutmeg
⅛ teaspoon allspice
⅛ teaspoon cloves
1½ cups half-and half or 1
   twelve-ounce can evaporated
   milk
1 teaspoon vanilla
1 cup pecans
2 tablespoons rum

Preheat oven to 425°F.

Prepare pumpkin or squash and applesauce. In a bowl, beat together the eggs and sugar until light. Mix in the pumpkin or winter squash, applesauce, flour, salt, cinnamon, ginger, nutmeg, allspice, cloves, half-and-half and vanilla and blend thoroughly. Pour into pie shell. Arrange pecan halves attractively over top of filling. Bake in the lower third of oven for 20 minutes, then reduce oven heat to 350°F. and bake 30 to 35 minutes longer or until the filling is firm and a knife inserted 1 inch from the edge comes out clean. Cool on a wire rack. At serving time, warm rum in a small container suitable for pouring. Light the rum with a match and pour immediately while flaming over the pie. Serve with ice cream or whipped cream.

Serves 6 to 8.

HONEY-PUMPKIN BUTTER

This butter is smooth and rich-flavored but not too sweet or over-spicy. It is easy to make and tastes great on toast, muffins or pancakes.

2 cups cooked pumpkin, puréed
½ cup honey
1 teaspoon grated lemon rind
1 tablespoon lemon juice
1 teaspoon cinnamon
¼ teaspoon nutmeg
¼ teaspoon ginger
⅛ teaspoon cloves
¼ teaspoon salt

Combine all ingredients thoroughly. Simmer uncovered on low heat for 35 to 40 minutes, stirring frequently until quite thick—the same consistency as a stiff apple butter. To check, drop a spoonful on a chilled saucer. When as thick as you like it, ladle into jelly jars and refrigerate.

Makes 1¼ to 1½ cups.

PUMPKIN MUFFINS

Delicious with breakfast or as snacks.

2 cups unbleached white flour
2 teaspoons baking powder
1 tablespoon pumpkin pie spice mix
¼ teaspoon salt
2 eggs, slightly beaten
1 cup cooked mashed pumpkin (or winter squash), well drained
½ cup dark brown sugar, packed
4 tablespoons melted butter or margarine
½ cup unsweetened applesauce
¼ cup milk, at room temperature

Preheat oven to 400°.
Heavily grease a 12-cup muffin pan. Sift flour, baking powder, pumpkin pie spice and salt into a large bowl. In a separate bowl, beat together eggs, pumpkin, sugar, butter, applesauce and milk. Stir dry ingredients into the pumpkin mixture, just until they are combined—do not overmix. Spoon batter into muffin cups and bake until the muffins are golden, about 30 minutes. Serve warm or at room temperature.

Makes 1 dozen.

TOMATILLOS

GREEN GAZPACHO SALAD

Crunchy, cool, and really refreshing.

6 tomatillos, blanched in boiling
water for 3 minutes, then
coarsely chopped
1 clove garlic, finely chopped
2 medium cucumbers, peeled,
seeded and coarsely chopped
2 green bell peppers, seeded and
coarsely chopped
4 scallions, including part of the
tops, coarsely chopped
1 green Anaheim mild chile,
char/roasted, peeled, seeded
and coarsely chopped
¼ cup chopped fresh parsley
2 tablespoons wine vinegar
2 tablespoons olive oil
½ teaspoon Worcestershire sauce
⅛ teaspoon Tabasco sauce
½ teaspoon ground cumin
½ teaspoon salt
¼ teaspoon pepper
4 ripe tomatoes cut in thick slices

GARNISH:
sour cream

If using food processor to chop
vegetables, do not chop too fine.
Combine all ingredients except the
tomatoes. Mix well and then refrigerate for several hours to allow
flavors to blend. Taste for seasoning.
To serve, lay tomato slices on individual serving plates. Drain gazpacho
mixture and, using a slotted spoon,
spoon it on top of the tomato slices
on each plate. Garnish with a dollop
of sour cream if desired.

Makes 5 to 6 cups.

TOMATILLO SALSA

*Makes an excellent dip, or serve along
with barbecued chicken or fish.*

8 tomatillos, roasted and peeled
1 serrano chile, char/roasted,
peeled, seeded
¼ teaspoon or 1 small clove
garlic
1 or 2 scallions, coarsely
chopped
1 tablespoon lime juice
1 tablespoon chopped cilantro
salt and pepper to taste

In a blender or food processor, combine all ingredients except cilantro.
Chop very coarsely; do not over-
process. Add cilantro and salt and
pepper to taste.

Makes about 1¼ cups.

TOMATOES

SALSA CRUDA OR SALSA FRESCA

Nothing can substitute for freshly made salsa. Serve with chips, as a condiment, with grilled meat or poultry, or with rice and beans.

4 large tomatoes, peeled, cut
  into small dice
1 clove garlic, chopped
1 or 2 fresh jalapeño peppers,
  char/roasted and peeled, seeded
  and finely chopped
2 Anaheim or mild green chiles,
  char/roasted and peeled, seeded
  and finely chopped
6 scallions, finely chopped
1 tablespoon chopped parsley
½ teaspoon fresh oregano, finely
  chopped, or ¼ teaspoon dried
2 tablespoons lime juice
1 tablespoon fresh cilantro,
  finely chopped
pinch of sugar
salt and pepper to taste

Combine all the ingredients in a serving bowl. Season to taste with salt and pepper. Cover and set aside for several hours to allow flavors to blend. Before serving, drain off excess liquid.

Makes 3 to 4 cups.

BAKED FRESH TOMATOES

This juicy herb-scented casserole is delicious as a lunch or as light supper fare.

8 or 9 medium-sized ripe, fresh
  tomatoes (about 2½ pounds)
2 tablespoons minced onions
2 tablespoons finely chopped
  parsley
½ cup fresh finely chopped basil
2 tablespoons butter or
  margarine, cut into small pieces
¾ cup Mozzarella cheese cut
  into ½-inch cubes
¾ cup Cheddar cheese cut into
  ½-inch cubes
¼ teaspoon each salt and freshly
  ground pepper
1½ cups seasoned bread croutons

Preheat oven to 375°.
  Dip tomatoes for about 15 seconds in very hot water to loosen skins. Remove skins and quarter tomatoes. Place in a saucepan and cook over medium heat 3 minutes. Remove with a slotted spoon, reserving juice for other purposes.
  Grease a 2-quart casserole. Combine the tomatoes with onions, parsley, basil, butter, cheeses, salt, pepper and croutons in the casserole. Bake uncovered for 20 minutes. Serve hot or at room temperature.

Serves 4 to 6.

FIRE AND ICE
TOMATO SALAD

An old favorite that is perfect to serve with barbecued meals on a hot day.

6 large tomatoes, cut in thick
  wedges
1 large, sweet green (or red or
  yellow) pepper, sliced in rings
1 large red onion, sliced in thin
  rings
1 cucumber, scored and sliced
  thin
1 tablespoon chopped parsley

DRESSING:
½ cup vinegar
⅓ cup water
1 teaspoon celery seed
1½ teaspoons mustard seed
½ teaspoon salt
1 tablespoon sugar
dash of Tabasco sauce
⅛ teaspoon freshly ground
  pepper

OPTIONAL GARNISH:
1 avocado, cubed

Put the tomatoes, peppers, and onions in alternate layers in a salad bowl, reserving cucumber in a separate bowl. Combine dressing ingredients in a small saucepan. Bring to a boil and cook 1 minute. Pour over vegetables. Chill. Just before serving, add the sliced cucumbers and sprinkle the parsley over the top of the vegetables.

Serves 6 to 8.

GREEN TOMATO AND
APPLE CHUTNEY

A fine way to use early- and late-season green tomatoes. This chutney keeps well and goes beautifully with cold meats, cheese or chicken.

5 cups green tomatoes, coarsely
  chopped
3 cups peeled, cored and coarsely
  chopped apples—use Pippins
  or Granny Smiths if available
1 large red bell pepper, seeded
  and coarsely chopped
½ cup raisins
2 tablespoons finely chopped
  fresh ginger
2 cloves finely chopped garlic
½ teaspoon mustard seed
½ teaspoon ground cumin
1 teaspoon ground coriander
⅛ teaspoon nutmeg
⅛ teaspoon cayenne pepper
2 teaspoons salt
1 cup brown sugar, firmly packed
1 cup mild white or rice vinegar

In a large 4- or 5-quart saucepan, combine all ingredients. Bring to a boil and then simmer, stirring occasionally, for about 45 minutes or until mixture is thickened. Cool, then store in glass jars in the refrigerator or seal the jars and process in a hot-water bath for 10 minutes for half-pints and 15 minutes for pints. Let chutney mellow for a few days before serving.

Makes about 5 cups.

Fresh Tomato Sauce Santa Fe

A delicious, fast sauce for a high-summer spaghetti dinner. Needs no cooking and retains the ingredients' beautiful colors and fresh flavors.

4 large tomatoes, peeled, seeded and coarsely chopped
1 red onion, very finely chopped
2 jalapeño chiles, stemmed, seeded and finely chopped; roasted and peeled first if you have time
2 small cloves garlic, finely chopped
1 cup fresh mint leaves, finely chopped
2 tablespoons olive oil
2 tablespoons red wine vinegar
1 teaspoon salt
fresh ground pepper to taste
8 ounces dried linguini or spaghetti
½ cup freshly grated Parmesan or Asiago cheese

Combine vegetables and mint leaves in a large bowl. Mix together oil and vinegar and pour over vegetables. Salt and pepper to taste. Let stand at room temperature 30 minutes to 1 hour to mix and develop flavors. Cook linguini in boiling salted water, drain well and toss with fresh sauce. Serve immediately, passing the grated cheese.

Serves 4.

Tuscan Pizza

The rich concentrated sauce based on vine-ripened tomatoes makes this pizza extra special.

2 tablespoons olive oil
1 clove garlic, finely chopped
1 small onion, chopped
1 cup tomatoes, including their juice
¼ cup fresh basil, finely chopped
2 tablespoons fresh parsley, chopped
1 teaspoon fresh oregano, finely chopped
pinch (each) of salt, pepper, and sugar
prepared pizza crust or English muffins
olive oil
½ cup finely shredded prosciutto or ham
½ cup grated Mozzarella cheese
¼ cup freshly grated Parmesan or Asiago cheese

Preheat oven to 400°.

In a small skillet, heat the oil, add garlic and onion, and sauté several minutes until fragrant and softened. Add tomatoes, then cover and simmer for 5 minutes. Uncover; add fresh herbs and a pinch each of salt, pepper and sugar. Cook over high heat, stirring until liquid is absorbed. Brush ready-to-use pizza crust or English muffins lightly with oil, then spread the tomato sauce over the top(s). Sprinkle with the prosciutto and cheeses. Bake on upper rack of oven for 5 to 8 minutes until bubbly and serve immediately.

Serves 4 to 6.

WATERCRESS

WALDORF-CRESS SALAD

A tangy salad with the sweetness of apple and bite of the cress.

VINAIGRETTE DRESSING:
Combine ingredients
thoroughly:
¼ cup wine vinegar
2 tablespoons lemon juice
½ teaspoon sugar
¾ teaspoon Dijon-style prepared
  mustard
½ cup light olive oil or salad oil

SALAD INGREDIENTS:
2 large, firm Red Delicious or
  other similar sweet red apples,
  cored and cut into ½-inch dice
⅓ cup Roquefort cheese,
  crumbled
⅓ cup coarsely chopped toasted
  walnuts
1 large bunch broadleaf cress
  or watercress, tough stems
  removed from watercress
½ head lettuce (romaine as first
  choice), washed and torn into
  small pieces

Toss apples, Roquefort cheese and
walnuts in a small bowl and spoon 2
tablespoons of the vinaigrette dressing over the apple mixture. Mix
well. To serve, add apple-cheese-nut
mixture to cress and lettuce. Add 2
to 3 tablespoons more dressing and
toss. Taste and add more dressing if
desired.

Serves 4.

WATERCRESS-EGGDROP SOUP

A light and quickly prepared Chinese-style soup that really takes advantage of watercress' special flavor.

- 4 tablespoons chopped or ground pork (turkey also can be used)
- 2 tablespoons soy sauce
- 1/3 cup finely sliced celery—slice on diagonal
- 1/3 cup canned water chestnuts, drained and thinly sliced
- 2 scallions, thinly sliced
- 1 quart (4 cups) chicken broth
- 1 egg, beaten
- 1 cup fresh chopped broadleaf cress or watercress, packed in cup
- optional: 1/2 cup tofu, diced in 1/2-inch cubes

Combine meat with soy sauce and let them marinate briefly while cutting up vegetables. Bring broth to a boil and add the marinated meat. Reduce to a simmer and cook 5 minutes. Add all the prepared vegetables. Bring back to a boil and add beaten egg slowly in a steady stream so it forms thin ribbons. Remove from heat, stir and add watercress. Serve immediately.

Serves 4 to 6.

SWEET AND SOUR WATERCRESS SALAD

The mild peppery bite of watercress is perfectly balanced by the hint of spicy sweetness in the dressing.

DRESSING:
- 2 tablespoons lemon juice
- 1/4 cup tarragon vinegar
- 1/4 cup catsup
- 1 tablespoon plus 2 teaspoons sugar
- 1/2 teaspoon salt
- 1 teaspoon prepared mustard
- 1 teaspoon Worcestershire sauce
- 1/2 cup vegetable oil

SALAD INGREDIENTS:
- 2 large bunches of watercress, washed and torn, tough stems removed
- large lettuce leaves to line individual salad plates

Whisk together all the dressing ingredients and toss a portion of the dressing with watercress leaves. (Reserve extra dressing for other salads.) Line each salad plate with a lettuce leaf and mound watercress salad in the center of each leaf to make individual salads.

Serves 6.

HERBS & EDIBLE FLOWERS

*H*aving easy access to the aromas and flavors of fresh herbs in abundance is one of the best rewards of being a kitchen gardener. Properly used, their bright perfumes excite and stimulate our sense of taste and smell.

Edible flowers combine both the ornamental and edible and open up a whole new aspect of gardening and cooking for both the eye and the palate. They will add elegance to a new dish or a quick pick-me-up to the appearance and flavor of everyday cooking. A standard caution: only certain flowers are edible—pick and use only flowers we identify here or that you have personally verified to be edible from an authoritative source. Use only blossoms you know haven't been sprayed, as most chemicals registered strictly for ornamentals are toxic.

Over the last decade cooks have abandoned the traditional canons of using certain herbs only with certain foods. We invite you to do the same! Start out with time-honored pairings but then experiment. For example, rosemary is wonderful with traditional partners chicken and white wine, but a pinch of its pungent piney flavor also lends sparkle to a big bowl of slightly sweetened fresh strawberries! Use herbs with a subtle hand: it is better to begin with too little and add more to taste. Try to add herbs the last ten minutes of cooking so as to preserve their oils.

Preserve your harvests either by freezing in heavy-duty plastic bags or try microwave drying (see page 79). Store in a cool, dry place out of sunlight. Most important, locate your herb garden in an easily accessible place so you'll be motivated to harvest and use fresh herbs in everyday cooking.

HERBS

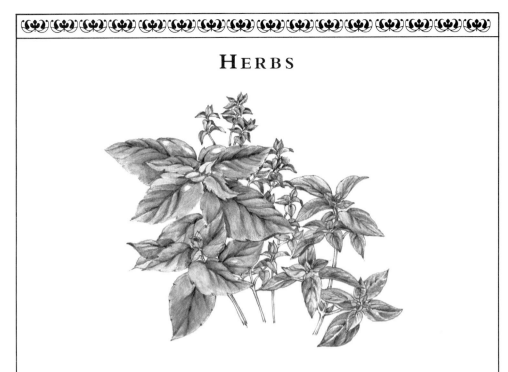

MICROWAVE HERB DRYING

A quick and easy way to preserve fresh herbs.

Easy to do! Pick sprigs of fresh herbs, and, if necessary, rinse and pat or air dry. Separate leaves from stems and measure 2 cups of leaves. Spread leaves evenly, in a thin layer, on a double thickness of paper towels. Microwave on high setting for a minimum of four and a maximum of six minutes. Check and stir the leaves several times during the drying process. When done, the herb leaves should be very brittle and quite crispy feeling when stirred with your fingers. *Note that processing time may vary slightly depending on your individual microwave, so experiment the first few times, watching carefully so you do not overdry.* Let dried leaves cool completely and then store them whole or crumbled in airtight containers in a cool dry place.

HERB MUSTARD VINAIGRETTE SALAD

Dijon mustard and fresh herbs are natural flavor enhancers in this delicious dressing that is perfect with all greens and terrific on ripe tomato slices.

  1 clove garlic, halved
  ¼ teaspoon salt
  2 teaspoons Dijon-style mustard
  2 tablespoons lemon juice
  1 tablespoon rice vinegar or
    other very mild vinegar
  2 tablespoons white wine
  6 tablespoons olive oil
  1 pinch sugar
  fresh ground pepper
  1 teaspoon chopped fresh herbs
    (your choice)
  assorted fresh salad greens

In a salad bowl, rub the garlic into the salt. Add mustard, lemon juice, vinegar and wine. Whisk in the oil. Add sugar, pepper and herbs. Remove garlic. Whisk again. Add salad greens and toss.

Makes ⅔ cup dressing.

BASIL-ROSEMARY CHICKEN WINGS

*For hors d'oeuvres or a tasty light meal.
We find these spicy tidbits are delicious
eaten cold the next day too, so make a
double recipe!*

**2 pounds chicken wings (about
24) prepared as "drumettes" if
available. Otherwise cut off
wing tips and cut wings at the
joint to create 2 winglets.**

MARINADE:
1 lemon
2 cloves garlic, finely chopped
2 tablespoons butter
2 tablespoons olive oil
3 tablespoons white wine
½ teaspoon fresh ground pepper
**1 teaspoon fresh rosemary,
crumbled, or ½ teaspoon dried**
¼ cup chopped fresh basil
½ teaspoon salt

GARNISH:
fresh basil sprigs.

Preheat oven to 425°.
   Grate 1 tablespoon lemon zest
(yellow part only of skin) and put
into a small heavy saucepan. Squeeze
the juice from the lemon into the
pan. Add remaining marinade ingredients, heat, and then simmer for 5
minutes. Pour marinade over chicken
wings and toss. Marinate at least ½
hour to blend flavors. Bake the
chicken wings on a baking sheet in
the preheated oven for 20–25 minutes
until glazed and browned. Garnish
with fresh basil sprigs. Can also be
barbecued over moderately hot
coals. Serve warm or cold.

Serves 6 to 8.

SWEET PEPPER AND BASIL STACKS

*Lovely to look at and eat. Makes a very
successful and light first course or salad.*

**4 large sweet red or yellow or
orange peppers**
4 large lettuce leaves
light olive oil
8–10 large fresh basil leves
**4–6 ounces Feta cheese (or fresh
chèvre)**

Char/roast the peppers; put in plastic
or paper bag. Cool 5 minutes. Skin
and seed and cut in half lengthwise.
Put lettuce leaves on individual salad
plates. Lay ½ pepper on each plate
and drizzle with olive oil. Cover
each pepper half with a layer of basil
leaves, then thin slices of cheese.
Sprinkle with a bit more oil. Top
each salad with the other pepper half
and sprinkle oil over each stack to
finish.

Serves 4.

Lemon Thyme- or Basil-Stuffed Chicken Breasts

A light, creamy and savory summer dinner treat. The perfume of the fresh herbs combines beautifully with the chicken and "light" cream cheese.

6 chicken breast halves, skinned and boned
½ cup "light" cream cheese
4 or 5 finely chopped scallions
14 to 16 fresh basil leaves or 6 teaspoons lemon thyme leaves
½ teaspoon salt
½ teaspoon pepper
1 teaspoon paprika
⅓ cup flour
2 eggs beaten with 2 teaspoons water
½ cup dried bread crumbs
½ cup freshly grated Parmesan or Swiss cheese
2 tablespoons melted butter or oil

Preheat oven to 350°.

Place each chicken breast in a plastic bag or between sheets of waxed paper and pound with a mallet or the edge of a saucer until just ⅛ inch thick. Roll each breast with a rolling pin to even and flatten. Spread one rounded tablespoon of the cream cheese down the center of each chicken piece. Sprinkle some of the chopped scallions and arrange basil leaves over the top of the whole flattened breast. If using lemon thyme, sprinkle 1 teaspoon of leaves over the cheese on each breast. Roll up jelly-roll fashion, tucking sides under. In a shallow pan, combine the salt, pepper, paprika and flour. Pour the beaten egg mixture into a second pan. In a third shallow pan, combine the crumbs and the grated cheese. Dip the rolled-up breasts first in the flour mixture, then the beaten eggs, and finish with a good coating of the crumb mixture. Place chicken on a greased baking sheet in a single layer and drizzle the melted butter over the tops of the breasts. Bake 20 to 25 minutes and serve immediately.

Serves 6.

PERSIAN MEATBALLS

*The mint and basil add a special flavor to this hearty main dish
everyone will thoroughly enjoy served over rice or couscous grains.*

MEATBALLS:
2 slices bread; milk to cover them
1 pound lean ground lamb or
  beef
½ teaspoon each salt and pepper
2 teaspoons finely chopped fresh
  mint
2 teaspoons finely chopped
  cinnamon basil
1 clove finely chopped garlic
1 teaspoon lemon juice
1 medium onion finely chopped
2 tablespoons freshly grated
  Parmesan or Asiago cheese
¼ cup red wine
olive oil for sautéing

SAUCE:
1 teaspoon flour
1 eight-ounce can tomato sauce
2 tablespoons red wine
½ large or 1 small bay leaf

GARNISH:
2 teaspoons chopped fresh mint

Soak bread in enough milk to cover
until milk is absorbed. Squeeze out
excess, then crumble soaked bread
into small pieces. Combine with all
other meatball ingredients and shape
into walnut-sized balls. Chill. Heat
oil in large skillet. Brown meatballs
evenly and remove from pan. Drain
fat. Add the teaspoon of flour to pan
and mix in tomato sauce slowly.
Add wine and bay leaf and heat to
simmer. Transfer meatballs back to
pan; cook over low heat until done
to your liking. To serve, remove bay
leaf and garnish with chopped mint
before serving.

Serves 4 to 6.

HERBED FRESH MUSHROOM PÂTÉ

This fine appetizer has a rich taste and meaty texture.

1 pound fresh mushrooms
2 tablespoons butter
½ cup finely chopped onion
½ teaspoon salt
2 teaspoons fresh thyme, finely chopped
⅛ teaspoon pepper
1 tablespoon brandy
2 hard-cooked eggs
1 teaspoon lemon juice
2 tablespoons mayonnaise
2 tablespoons finely chopped parsley
crackers or melba toast

Rinse, pat dry and finely chop mushrooms, or coarsely grate in food processor. In a large skillet, melt butter. Add mushrooms, onion, salt, thyme and pepper. Cook over moderate heat, stirring often, until all liquid has evaporated, about 10 minutes. Add brandy. Cook, stirring constantly, until brandy evaporates, about 1 minute. Cool. Reserve 1 egg yolk. Finely chop remaining 1 whole egg and 1 egg white. Add to mushroom mixture with lemon juice, mayonnaise and parsley. Mix well. Turn into a 1½-cup container. Cover and chill. At serving time, pack into small serving dish or unmold onto lettuce on a serving plate. Using a small fine mesh sieve held directly over serving bowl or molded mushroom mixture, sieve reserved egg yolk over top. Serve with crackers or melba toast.

Serves 8 to 10 as an appetizer.

GLAZED FRUITED CHICKEN WITH ROSEMARY

The aromatic, piney scent of rosemary sets off the glazed dried fruits beautifully in this very satisfying main dish.

4 chicken breasts, halved
4 chicken thighs
salt and pepper or seasoned salt
1 clove garlic, finely chopped

SAUCE:
1 cup water
1 cup dry white wine
2 tablespoons lemon juice
¼ cup honey
2 teaspoons hot dry mustard
2 teaspoons fresh rosemary, finely chopped, or 1 teaspoon dried
½ cup pitted prunes
½ cup dried apricots
1 large fresh apple, cored and sliced into rings

GARNISH:
chopped parsley

Preheat oven to 350.
Sprinkle chicken pieces with salt and pepper. Rub with garlic. Place in a 9 × 13-inch baking pan, skin side up. Bake 45 minutes. While chicken is baking, prepare sauce. In a saucepan, combine water, wine, lemon juice, honey, mustard and rosemary. Bring mixture to a boil and simmer 15 minutes. Add prunes, apricots and apple slices and simmer another 15 minutes or until liquid is reduced by half and fruit is tender. Remove chicken from oven. Pour off fat and skin chicken if desired. Spoon fruit sauce over chicken. Turn oven temperature up to 400. Return chicken to oven and bake for 15 minutes longer, basting once or twice. Sprinkle with chopped parsley. Serve hot with noodles or rice.

Serves 6.

MARTY'S BASIL-RICE SALAD

A hearty and satisfying main dish salad for a hot day. This salad will also complement grilled meats and poultry nicely, or take it along to a barbecue picnic.

DRESSING:
Combine and mix together:
2 tablespoons lemon juice
2 tablespoons red wine vinegar
¼ teaspoon each salt and freshly
  ground pepper
2 tablespoons fresh parsley, finely
  chopped
½ cup finely chopped fresh basil
1 clove garlic, finely chopped
¼ cup plus 1 tablespoon olive oil

SALAD:
¼ cup scallions, finely chopped
1½ cups cooked kidney beans (or
  1 can, drained)
3 cups cooked rice
2 large carrots, shredded
2 tomatoes, halved and cut into
  thin slices

Mix together the scallions, beans, rice and carrots. Mound evenly in serving platter, then arrange tomato slices around the edge. Pour dressing evenly over salad and let the flavors blend for ½ hour. Serve either at room temperature or slightly chilled.

Serves 6 to 8.

SHAKER HERB BLENDS

Here are some good herb combinations to have on hand at the table if you are trying to cut down on salt.

Combine:
2 parts mild dried and crumbled
herbs; your choice of:
    basil
    summer savory
    lemon thyme
    dill
    parsley
    sweet marjoram
1 part stronger herbs:
    rosemary
    oregano
    sage
    Amsterdam cutting celery

Whirl very briefly in a blender or crumble together with your fingers. Keep on the table in a little bowl or a shaker with big holes. Optional additional seasoning: sesame seeds.

Anise Hyssop Carrots

The delicate sweet anise flavor complements the crunchy carrots in a delightful way.

>   1 to 2 tablespoons butter
>   2 tablespoons water
>   1 pound carrots, very thinly
>   sliced
>   3 tablespoons fresh anise hyssop
>   leaves, very finely chopped
>   1 tablespoon lemon juice
>   optional: salt to taste

In a saucepan, melt butter, add water, and steam carrots, chopped anise hyssop and lemon juice for 6 to 10 minutes, just until tender but still crisp. Salt to taste. Serve immediately.

Serves 4 to 6.

Minted Melon

Easy to make, this elegantly simple melon dish is a refreshing treat on a hot summer day.

>   1 orange-fleshed melon, seeded
>   and flesh cut into large cubes
>   1 teaspoon grated orange rind
>   ¼ cup orange juice
>   2 tablespoons sugar
>   ⅓ cup Shepherd's Perseus
>   Raspberry Vinegar
>   ¼ cup finely chopped *fresh* mint

Put melon cubes in an attractive serving bowl. Combine other ingredients and mix well to dissolve sugar. Pour over melon. Chill covered for an hour to let flavors blend.

Serves 4.

Marinated Anise Hyssop Baked Chicken

The flavors of ginger and anise hyssop add a delicious perfume to this fine chicken dish.

>   1 cut-up frying chicken, 2½–3½
>   pounds

>   MARINADE:
>   1 tablespoon chopped fresh
>   ginger
>   1 cup finely chopped anise hyssop
>   leaves and flowers
>   1 teaspoon cinnamon
>   3 cloves garlic, minced
>   3 tablespoons oil
>   3 tablespoons soy sauce

Mix marinade ingredients together and pour over the chicken right in the baking pan. Let marinate for 2 to 4 hours. Bake at 375° for 45 minutes or until chicken is cooked and nicely browned.

Serves 3 or 4.

CORIANDER SPICE CAKE

This is a moist, delicate cake that keeps very well and actually improves in flavor the second and third day—if it lasts that long. A good way to use your coriander seed harvest.

2½ cups sifted all-purpose flour
2 teaspoons soda
1 teaspoon salt
2 teaspoons ground ginger
1 teaspoon ground cloves
1 teaspoon cinnamon
1 teaspoon dried coriander seeds, crushed to a powder, or 1 teaspoon ground
½ cup sugar
½ cup butter, melted
1 cup molasses
2 eggs, slightly beaten
½ cup raisins
½ cup chopped walnuts
⅓ cup chopped candied orange peel
1 cup boiling water

ORANGE BUTTER ICING

1 pound sifted powdered sugar
¼ teaspoon salt
½ cup butter, at room temperature
3 to 4 tablespoons orange juice
2 teaspoons grated orange peel (zest)

Preheat oven to 350°.

Grease a 9 × 13-inch baking pan. Sift flour, soda, salt and all the spices together. In a bowl blend sugar with melted butter. Beat in molasses and eggs. Stir in raisins, walnuts and orange peel. Add sifted dry ingredients and hot water alternately to egg mixture, beating after each addition until just combined. Don't overmix. Pour into baking pan and bake for 30 minutes or until a cake tester inserted in center comes out clean. Sprinkle with confectioners' sugar or top with our Orange Butter Icing.

Sift powdered sugar into mixer bowl, add salt and mix. Beat in the butter and add the orange juice a tablespoon at a time until you reach the desired consistency. Add orange-peel zest and frost cooled cake.

Lemon Thyme Bread

A light-textured teabread—great for afternoon snacks. Keeps well and elegantly satisfies afternoon cravings.

> 2 cups unbleached all-purpose flour
> 2 teaspoons baking powder
> 1/4 teaspoon salt
> 6 tablespoons butter or margarine, at room temperature
> 1 cup sugar
> 2 eggs
> 1 tablespoon grated lemon rind
> 2 tablespoons lemon juice
> 2 tablespoons finely chopped lemon thyme
> 2/3 cup milk
>
> LEMON GLAZE:
> 2 tablespoons lemon juice mixed with about 1/2 cup powdered sugar or enough to make a thin, pourable consistency

Preheat oven to 325°.

Grease and flour an 8 × 4-inch loaf pan. On a sheet of waxed paper, sift together flour, baking powder and salt. In a bowl cream butter; gradually add sugar, beating until fluffy. Add eggs one at a time, beating well after each addition. Mix in lemon rind, lemon juice and lemon thyme. Add dry ingredients alternately with milk, mixing just until batter is smooth and blended. Pour batter into pan. Bake for 55 to 60 minutes or until a wooden pick inserted in center of bread comes out clean. Let stand in pan for 5 minutes. Turn out and slowly pour lemon glaze over the loaf.

Fresh Apple Cake with Lemon Thyme

A good apple cake elevated to something special with the addition of the lemon thyme. Tastes good the first day and mellows beautifully if made ahead.

> 2 large tart apples, unpeeled, cut into 1/2-inch cubes—about 2 1/2 cups
> 2 1/2 tablespoons finely chopped lemon thyme leaves
> 1 tablespoon lemon juice
> 1 cup sugar
> 1 1/2 cups flour
> 1 teaspoon baking powder
> 1/2 teaspoon baking soda
> 1/4 teaspoon salt
> 1/2 cup chopped nuts (optional)
> 2 eggs, lightly beaten
> 6 tablespoons butter, melted and cooled
> 1 teaspoon vanilla

Preheat oven to 350°.

Grease and flour an 8 × 8 × 2-inch baking pan. Combine apples, lemon thyme, lemon juice and 1/2 cup of the sugar in a bowl and set aside. Sift together flour, baking powder, soda and salt. Add remaining 1/2 cup sugar and optional nuts if used. Set aside. Beat eggs with melted butter and vanilla. Add apple–lemon thyme mixture, mixing until blended. Add dry ingredients, stirring until just combined. Spoon batter into prepared pan and bake 35 minutes or until cake tester comes out clean. Allow to cool and serve.

EDIBLE FLOWERS

BLOSSOM TEA SANDWICHES

*Open-faced finger sandwiches that offer a handsome smorgasbord of colors and flavors.
Decorate each sandwich with several savory edible flower petals and herb blossoms
and serve. Expect to be applauded for your artistry!*

**1 large cucumber, peeled, seeded
and finely chopped
1 eight-ounce package of cream
cheese ("light" style okay), at
room temperature
¾ teaspoon Worcestershire sauce
¼ teaspoon minced garlic
1 teaspoon salt
¼ cup finely chopped chives or
scallions
thinly sliced cracked wheat or
white bread, crusts removed
lots of edible blossoms:
nasturtium blossoms, chive
blossoms, borage flowers,
calendula petals, pea or bean
flowers, herb blossoms, rinsed
and patted down**

Squeeze chopped cucumber in a
kitchen towel to remove as much
moisture as possible; set aside. Blend
together the cream cheese, seasonings and chives or scallion. Add
cucumber and combine well but do
not overmix. Spread on bread and
cut into finger-sized open sandwiches. To serve: decorate the tops
of the sandwiches with petals of
various edible flowers, combining
colors and shapes to suit your palate
and your fancy.

CALENDULA LEMON PUDDING CAKE

A tempting dessert with lovely lemon flavors.
Not at all rich, so you can indulge yourself!

¾ cup sugar
¼ cup all-purpose unbleached
  flour
⅛ teaspoon salt
2 tablespoons melted butter
1 tablespoon grated lemon rind
5 tablespoons lemon juice
3 egg yolks
1½ cups milk
3 egg whites, at room
  temperature
⅛ teaspoon cream of tartar
¼ cup sugar
6 tablespoons calendula petals

GARNISH:
calendula petals
whipped cream

Preheat oven to 350°. Lightly grease a 1½-quart baking dish or 6 custard cups. Set into a slightly larger pan, at least 2 inches deep.

In a mixing bowl, combine the ¾ cup sugar, flour and salt. Add butter, lemon rind, and lemon juice and mix until thoroughly blended. With a whisk beat egg yolks until thick and lemon-colored; add milk and mix well. Combine with lemon mixture, stirring until blended.

In another bowl, beat egg whites until foamy, add cream of tartar and beat until soft peaks form. Add the ¼ cup of sugar gradually and beat until stiff but not dry. Fold the whites and calendula petals into lemon mixture. Spoon into baking dish or custard cups. Pour 1 inch of hot water around them.

Bake until set and top is golden brown, about 35 minutes for custard cups or 45 minutes for baking dish. Remove from water and let cool on a wire rack. Serve warm or chilled with a dollop of whipped cream and a sprinkle of additional calendula petals.

Serves 6.

GENERAL USES OF HERBS

Beef garlic and regular chives, marjoram, oregano, savory, thyme

Breads lemon basil, coriander, dill, marjoram, oregano, thyme

Cheese basil, garlic and regular chives, chervil, dill, fennel, thyme

Eggs basil, chervil, garlic and regular chives, oregano, parsley, tarragon

Fish anise and lemon basil, chervil, garlic and regular chives, dill, fennel, parsley, tarragon, thyme

Fruit anise, cinnamon and lemon basils, ground coriander seed

Lamb arugula, lemon basil, garlic chives, marjoram, mint, oregano, thyme (*make little slits in the lamb and insert herbs before cooking*)

Pork coriander/cilantro, garlic chives, sage, savory, thyme

Poultry scented basils, regular and garlic chives, oregano, sage, savory, thyme

Salads basil, chervil, garlic and regular chives, cilantro, dill, marjoram, parsley, savory, sorrel (*all can also be made into herb vinegars for extra flavor*)

Soups basil, garlic and regular chives, dill, marjoram, parsley, savory, thyme

Vegetables basils, chervil, regular and garlic chives, dill, marjoram, oregano, parsley, savory, tarragon, thyme

RECIPE INDEX

An Invitation to Our Readers

We'd like to send you a complimentary copy of our complete 112-page seed catalog. We feature over 350 varieties of fine vegetables, culinary herbs and specialty flower seeds as well as collections of seeds for different cuisines. The catalog includes helpful growing information and carefully chosen recipes for enjoying the garden's bounty.

Simply fill in your name and address on the back of this card and return it to us. We will mail your catalog promptly via first class mail.

Best Regards,

Renee Shepherd

An Invitation to Our Readers

We'd like to send you a complimentary copy of our complete 112-page seed catalog. We feature over 350 varieties of fine vegetables, culinary herbs and specialty flower seeds as well as collections of seeds for different cuisines. The catalog includes helpful growing information and carefully chosen recipes for enjoying the garden's bounty.

Simply fill in your name and address on the back of this card and return it to us. We will mail your catalog promptly via first class mail.

Best Regards,

Renee Shepherd

SHEPHERD'S
GARDEN SEEDS

Please send a complimentary copy of your catalog.

Name

Address

City   State   Zip

6116 Highway 9, Felton, CA 95018, (408) 335-5400

SHEPHERD'S
GARDEN SEEDS

Please send a complimentary copy of your catalog.

Name

Address

City   State   Zip

6116 Highway 9, Felton, CA 95018, (408) 335-5400